T0021698

FINISH
the
RACE

Insight Into Fighting
The Good Fight of Faith
And Finishing Well

KINGSLEY OSEI

WestBow
PRESS®
A DIVISION OF THOMAS NELSON
& ZONDERVAN

WestBow Press books may be ordered through booksellers or by contacting:

WestBow Press
A Division of Thomas Nelson & Zondervan
1663 Liberty Drive
Bloomington, IN 47403
www.westbowpress.com
844-714-3454

Scripture quotations are taken from the New King James Version®. Copyright
© 1982 by Thomas Nelson. Used by permission. All rights reserved.

ISBN: 978-1-6642-4701-7 (sc)
ISBN: 978-1-6642-4700-0 (e)

Print information available on the last page.

WestBow Press rev. date: 10/11/2021

TABLE OF CONTENTS

INTRODUCTION

"But none of these things move me; nor do I count my life dear to myself, so that I may finish my race with joy, and the ministry which I received from the Lord Jesus, to testify to the gospel of the grace of God". – **Acts 20:24**

The apostle Paul was a great man with great accomplishments. He concluded his life on the earth by proclaiming that his greatest achievement was to fulfill his purpose according to the will of God. He said he considered his former life before Christ no matter how great it may have been, as "loss" and "count them rubbish". He came to that conclusion for one reason; "that I may gain Christ".

"But what things were gain to me, these I have counted loss for Christ. Yet indeed I also count all things loss for the excellence of the knowledge of Christ Jesus my Lord, for whom I have suffered the loss of all things, and count them as rubbish, that I may gain Christ" – **Philippians 3:7-8**

Wow! What a thought and conclusion! The big question is, what made such a great man arrive at such a conclusion? What did he come to find out? What did he learn or come to a realization of, that brought him to such summarization of his life?

Paul did not make such a statement because he had unintentionally lost what he had gained. He simply considered those things, which he had gained as non-entities in his life due to the precious value of his rebirthed experience and journey with God. This is a person who understood both the vanity of the world without God in contrast to the value of the Kingdom of God. He also regarded his former life as "rubbish" or "junk". This is a well thought out and defined conclusion of the preciousness of living a life on this earth with both the revelation of Christ and a relationship with Him. The greatest life on this earth is a blessed life through Christ.

> *"The blessing of the LORD makes one rich, and He adds no sorrow with it."* – **Proverbs 10:22**

One can have all the wealth of this earth but still, live in the deepest sorrow and despair. The true joy and fulfillment of this life was not intended to be rooted in the material possessions of this world, neither was it intended to be intrinsically inherited in the mere accomplishment of life. Although riches make life easy in many aspects, joy and fulfillment come in a much steeper and deeper revelation in this life. The Lord Jesus Himself asked this profound question.

> *"For what profit is it to a man if he gains the whole world, and loses his own soul?"* – **Matthew 16:26**

What a profound inquiry to ponder upon! This is the revelation that Paul had. Anyone who genuinely ponders upon such a sincere question should arrive safely at Paul's newfound truth and understanding when he said he considered any life no matter the accomplishment without Christ as "lost" and "rubbish", or "junk". Your life without Christ as the core and the center is a lost cause and rubbish. Paul gave up everything in order to not just finish his life on this earth with Christ at the core, but also to fulfill the assignment that Jesus had called him to and the destiny that God created him for. Paul said, "finish the race". As humans, you were designed by the Creator for His pleasure.

"You are worthy, O Lord, to receive glory and honor and power; for You created all things, and by Your pleasure, they exist and were created." - **Revelation 4:11**

It is important to note the timing and positioning of the aforementioned Scripture. The passage is strategically stated in the latter book of the Word of God. It is the summarization of those who understand why they were given the wonderful opportunity of life on this earth. They had the precious revelation that no matter what was afforded to them on this earth, their life on this earth had a divine purpose, and that purpose is connected to the very Being who created them. They understood that their life on this earth was not an accident and neither was it a fluke. They discovered the truth of why they were created and lived according to that very truth.

For: My beloved and precious wife – Rita and my precious jewels of life Sephora, Laurelle and Andrea.

WORTH FIGHTING

In **2 Timothy 4:7,** Paul boldly stated,

> *"I have fought the good fight, I have finished the*
> *race, I have kept the faith."*

Paul was always a successful man in his personal endeavors. He was successful both when he was a non-believer of Christ and when he became born again. He always had the zeal to win. He gained extensive notoriety even above his peers and contemporaries. He was very successful both in his personal life as well as in his religious pursuit. In his personal life, he was a highly educated man astute in commerce. On the other hand, he hated the church in his religious pursuit. He was a Pharisee who detested Christ and anyone that followed Christ. He said of himself,

> *"If anyone else thinks he may have confidence in*
> *the flesh, I more so: circumcised the eighth day,*
> *of the stock of Israel, of the tribe of Benjamin, a*
> *Hebrew of the Hebrews; concerning the law, a*
> *Pharisee; concerning zeal, persecuting the church;*

1

concerning the righteousness which is in the law, blameless". – **Philippians 3:4-6**

God's plans for our lives are always in effect, even before we become aware of His purpose for our lives. During the course of Paul's life on this earth, whether he was aware or not, he was always on course to be plugged into the purpose of God. The outcome of God's intention was going to be contingent upon how Paul was going to respond. In Paul's position, all he needed was a revelation of Christ in order for that incredible reversal of heart to occur. God does not save anyone, so that they will be a lump on a log. God has saved you, to be part of His divine plan on this earth. Even before you became aware of Him, he had already orchestrated a unique role for you within His purpose. He has a plan for you to be an important part of the ministry of reconciliation and to give aid in bringing His people into their God-given destiny. You are an important part of God's big plan!

> *"Now all things are of God, who has reconciled us to Himself through Jesus Christ, and has given us the ministry of reconciliation, that is, that God was in Christ reconciling the world to Himself, not imputing their trespasses to them, and has committed to us the word of reconciliation."*
> – **2 Corinthians 5:18-19**

The onset of God's plan for your life is in being discovered by Christ, discovering yourself in Him, and in your total surrender to Him. When you meet Christ through the revelation of His Spirit, that is when your true life, in addition to true living, starts. Jesus is the only way into anything that you would like to transcend into eternity. Although Paul had many great accolades in comparison to his contemporaries, he described his life with Christ and God's purpose for his life as "the race" and "the good fight", which takes precedence over all else. He had more value in his life with Christ than his past life that was without Christ, no matter how earthly glorious it was. This is an astounding claim considering the fact that his credits included being a Roman Citizen along with many other great accomplishments. In those days, being a Jew with Roman citizenship was a prime position to be in. We see the value in this assertion in **Acts 22,** when his citizenship aided him from being punished by Roman soldiers for doing the work of God. In the chapter (**verse 28**), the Roman commander indicated that he bought his citizenship with a "large sum of money" and Paul responded that he was actually a citizen by birth. Paul was born a Roman Citizen (**Acts 22:25-28**). Although being a Roman citizen for a Jew was a great thing to boast about, Paul would rather be a citizen of the Kingdom of Heaven. He boasted,

> *"For our citizenship is in heaven, from which we also eagerly wait for the Savior, the Lord Jesus Christ."* – **Philippians 3:20**

The value of Paul's statement is both bold and vivid considering what Roman citizenship meant in those times. His Roman citizenship aided him tremendously in doing the work of God. Paul counted his Roman citizenship as more valuable in the Kingdom of God, than outside of the Kingdom of God. Anything that you receive and use for the cause of God's Kingdom has more value than the riches of the world that are outside the Kingdom of God.

This is why Scripture says,

"Little that the righteous has, is better than the riches of many wicked." – **Psalms 37:16**

Paul understood that when you use your resources to advance the Kingdom of God, your life on earth will be protected and guarded by God, and you reap for yourself great reward in Heaven (**Matthew 6:19-21**). The desire to walk with Christ and to fully give yourself to Him and His cause permeates your life when you are in a place of knowing Christ as Paul did. There is an astounding reason why Scripture encourages you to imitate Paul as he imitated Christ (**1 Corinthians 11:1**). The deciding factor for Paul was his revelation of Christ. It is impossible to receive a true revelation of Christ and not give Him your all. Giving Christ your all will always produce a supernatural outcome in your life. It is a quest of sowing the natural aspect of your life, in order to receive the supernatural. The concept of sowing always produces more potential than the single seed that goes into the ground. Every seed carries more seed and bears a greater amount of fruit. However, that potential is not realized or apprehended until the seed is sown, and completely given up to the ground for the process as ordained by God (**John 12:24**). The same God who turns a single seed of any kind into a tree with plenty of fruits, can turn what you give over to Him into a strong tree of life. This transformation is not just for you, but for others near and afar; this is what happened with Paul. He gave his life and everything he had to Christ, and here we are after thousands of years, we are still talking about him and being blessed by His life. Paul is one example of many, both now and then. This amazing journey for

Paul started after his revelation of who Christ is. Do you want your life to be transformed? Pray for a deeper revelation of Christ through His Word and by His Spirit! Make a conscious decision and effort to be committed to what God is doing right now and in this generation! It always starts with a true revelation of Christ. Here is what Paul said in **Galatians 1:11-12,**

> *"But I make known to you, brethren, that the gospel which was preached by me is not according to man. For I neither received it from man, nor was I taught it, but it came through the <u>revelation of Jesus Christ</u>."*

The rejection of Christ is the lack of revelation of Christ. When you are at a place of lack of motivation, lack of commitment, lack of desire for the things of Christ, it is simply due to a lack of revelation of Christ. No one will ever receive a true revelation of who Christ is, become a true partaker of the heavenly calling, and at the same time desert Him and the Kingdom of God. There is an amazing and noteworthy event that took place in **Matthew16,** when Christ asked the disciples who they thought others were saying He was. Upon suggestive assertions from others, Peter eventually made a statement to which Christ confirmed in **verse 17. He confirmed,** that flesh and blood did not reveal this to Peter, but rather a power beyond Human abilities. This event was a monumental occurrence not only for the Kingdom of God, but also for Peter himself whom Christ at that declaration by Peter, affirmed him as the leader among the disciples of Christ. Jesus also declared that upon that revelation He will build His church. The revelation of Christ is what every person who seeks to run the faith race, needs to pursue and possess in this life. The more you know Christ, the more you will want to know Him; and the more you know Him, the more you will want to give your all for Him. Paul upon receiving the revelation of Christ used everything he had to advance the Gospel of Christ. Again, the more you know Him, the more you will love and serve Him. Paul's prestigious life afforded him to be trained during his Pharisaical order by the great Gamaliel. He described himself as having sat at the feet of this admired leader (**Acts 22:3**). Gamaliel's influence is evident in **Acts 5,** when he counseled a group of people and convinced them with both cognition and influence to refrain from killing the Apostles. He was a highly respected Pharisee. Gamaliel was from the highest lineage of honored Jewish Rabbins (Same as Rabbi). History and tradition credit him as the 35th receiver of the traditions and of the law given at Sinai (Received in 1446 BC). He succeeded his father, Rabbi Simeon, as president of Sanhedrin. The Sanhedrin was the religious court. Israel was commanded to obey every word of the Sanhedrin council. Paul's authority to condemn "People of the Way" was due to his strong connections under Gamaliel. Paul also had his own business in Tentmaking (Acts 18:2-3).

Tentmaking was a lucrative business during that era, as most of the population used tents for various functions and reasons. Also, as a Pharisee, Paul had to study the law thoroughly. The word "Pharisee" means "pure" and "separated" in the Hebrew language. They were the founders of Rabbinic Judaism. The loyalty of the Pharisees was to God's law and their sole purpose was for personal holiness. Pharisees studied from the age of 14 years to 40 years.

This means they were highly informed concerning the law and were fully equipped to ensure obedience to the law. The Lord Jesus described the Pharisee as,

> *"They sit on the seat of Moses"* so *"People must do what they ask but not to do what they do"*.
> – **Matthew 23:1-3**

Meaning, they knew the law in their minds, but they lacked the revelation of Christ through the Word. God had the intention of having His Word in their hearts and not in their minds.

> *"This is the covenant I will make with them after that time, says the Lord. I will put my laws in their hearts, and I will write them on their minds."*
> (**Jeremiah 31:33**; **Hebrews 10:16**).

Transformation does not come through the information in your mind. Transformation takes place through revelation. Revelation is when the Word of God sinks deep into your heart through the power and the work of the Holy Spirit. Paul along with the rest of the Pharisees had the law in their minds. They knew it inside out, but it was taking no effect in their life. Unless you allow the Word of God to sink into your heart and spirit, there will be no supernatural results in your life. In other words, you do not look for ways to debate your way out of His Word, but rather endeavor to obey and to be transformed by the power of the Word of God. Before his revelation of Christ, Paul had the authority to sanction the killings and imprisonment of the "People of the Way" (**Acts 26:9-11; Acts 22:4; Acts 7:54-60; 8:1-3**).

The summarization of these feats puts a good perspective on the influence that Paul had. Not to mention, that he also spoke all of the major languages of commerce in that era. He grew up speaking Aramaic because of his parents. Paul used the word "Maranatha" in **1 Corinthians 16:12**, which is Aramaic for "come Lord". He called Peter "Cephas", which means "Rock" in Aramaic (**Galatians 2:9, 1 Corinthians 9:5**; etc.). He spoke Greek (**Acts 21:37-39**), another incredible attribute considering the fact that education was a privilege afforded to few prominent families. He wrote his letters in Greek. Greek was the official language of the eastern Roman Empire. Paul also spoke Hebrew (**Acts 21:40; Acts 26:13-15**). He grew up speaking the peasant language of Aramaic. Jesus also grew up on this earth speaking Aramaic (**Mark 5:41** - Talitha Cumi "little girl"; **Matthew 27:46** – "Eli Eli lama sabachthani). Yet, when Jesus revealed Himself to Saul of Tarsus, He spoke Hebrew with him. According to **Galatians 1:13;14**, Paul advanced beyond his contemporaries. His religious reverence, social status, economical class and prestige, were embedded into one status of an incredible honor. Here is a very important observation to note....

Philippians 3:2-11.

"Beware of dogs, beware of evil workers, beware of the mutilation! For we are the circumcision, who worship God in the Spirit, rejoice in Christ Jesus, and have no confidence in the flesh, though I also might have confidence in the flesh. If anyone else thinks he may have confidence in the flesh, I more so: circumcised the eighth day, of the stock of Israel,

of the tribe of Benjamin, a Hebrew of the Hebrews; concerning the law, a Pharisee; concerning zeal, persecuting the church; concerning the righteousness which is in the law, blameless. But what things were gain to me, these I have counted loss for Christ. Yet indeed I also count all things loss for the excellence of the knowledge of Christ Jesus my Lord, for whom I have suffered the loss of all things, and count them as rubbish, that I may gain Christ and be found in Him, not having my own righteousness, which is from the law, but that which is through faith in Christ, the righteousness which is from God by faith; that I may know Him and the power of His resurrection, and the fellowship of His sufferings, being conformed to His death, if, by any means, I may attain to the resurrection from the dead."

Paul was excited and promoted his new found life and purpose in Christ over and above his former life. Paul spoke about his experience with Christ at every opportunity. The most powerful witnessing tool you have is your experience with Christ, which you receive through revelation. Paul's love for Christ and his commitment made him the second most influential person in the New Testament beside the Savior Jesus Christ, who lived on this earth as God incarnated. When Paul became born again, he did not rely on his own strength any longer. Although the natural accolades and accomplishments can give you aid in some circumstances, life is better when you tap into the supernatural source of God. Upon his salvation, Paul began to rely on the power of Christ instead of his own strength. He said in **Philippians 4:13** *"I can do all things through Christ who strengthens me"*.

This is one of the most exciting experiences, when a person walks with God and to the revelation of the truth. You too, can finish the race, because the strength that carries you through and gives you aid is not natural strength or human strength. You too, can do all things through Christ, who strengthens you. This amazing race of faith is not a battle for the strong, the poor, or the rich. It is a race of faith! All you have to do is have faith in God, trust in His Word and take it one step at a time. Not even Paul relied on his own strength. He needed the grace of God, and so do you. You can run this race and finish your course. Don't give up. Keep trusting!

YOU HAVE GOD

"It is God who works in you to will and to act in order to fulfill his good purpose" (**Philippians 2:13**).

His grace will always be sufficient for you, to carry you through. No matter who you are and how much you have accomplished on this earth, finishing your race and finishing it well will be the most important aspect of your life. What a remarkable feat to be able to circumvent life's trials, challenges, temptations and the hoopla. To be committed to the truth of Christ to a plateau where you are able to state with boldness that "to live is for Christ and to die is to gain". This is a position all should strive to be. So that you may be sure, Paul will show he navigated his final destination; stating it is never by his own strength. He urges you with this spiritual knowledge by saying, it is God who "works in you both to will and to do for His own good purpose" – **Philippians 2:13**, and by this he meant the Holy Spirit. Paul believed that He who lived in Him was greater than He who lives in the world. He relied on the strength of God. He said…

> *"I can do all things through Christ who strengthen me"* – **Philippians 4:13**

Relying on the strength of God through His Spirit and His Word is the only way that you will be able to finish your own race in Christ. Although like Paul, your personal accomplishments can open doors of opportunities for you, but it is your faith in God that will ultimately lead you and bring you to the finishing line of the faith race. In other words, the Kingdom of God that is in you must be more important to you than the world around you. You must see your journey in Christ as of more value than anything else around you. Not that other obligations and responsibilities are not important, but that Christ is of more value to you than any other ventures. Jesus gave a powerful inspiration through the intriguing story of the parable of the talent. In the end, the Lord desires to say to you "well done, good and faithful servant". Your utmost passion should be geared towards earnestly desiring to hear those very words from the good Master. In His efforts to give a deeper revelation of the vitality of doing all that is necessary to strive for those endearing words from the Master, Paul gave His all. Jesus Himself said in **Matthew 25:14-30,**

*"**The journey of the Kingdom is like a man traveling to a far country, who had called his servants and gave them his goods.** Some* translations will call it talent. It can also be interpreted as 'time'.

Jesus told that to *"one of the servants he gave five talents, to another two, and to another one, to each according to his own ability; and immediately he went on a journey...."*

In the story thus far, it is interesting that Jesus said they were all given the goods/talents "according to their own ability". Here, it is important to note that Jesus highlights the fact that you should never perceive what you go through in your faith race as something beyond strength or God's ability. If God allows it to come to you, He will give you the strength to get through it, and to come out stronger than before.

1 Corinthians 10:13 encourages you that, **"No temptation has overtaken you except such as is common to man; but God *is* faithful, who will not allow you to be tempted beyond what you are able, but with the temptation will also make the way of escape, that you may be able to bear** *it* **".**

The challenges of the journey are never greater than the Master of the journey. Jesus said,

> *"The one who had received the five talents went and traded with them, and made another five talents. And likewise he who had received two gained two more also. Jesus said, but the one who had received one went and dug in the ground, and hid his lord's money. Jesus said, after a long time the lord of those servants came and settled accounts with them.*

> *"So he who had received five talents came and brought five other talents, and said, 'Lord, you delivered to me five talents; look, I have gained five more talents besides them. His lord said to*

him, 'Well done, good and faithful servant; you were faithful over a few things, I will make you ruler over many things. Enter into the joy of your lord. He also who had received two talents came and said, 'Lord, you delivered to me two talents; look, I have gained two more talents besides them. His lord said to him, 'Well done, good and faithful servant; you have been faithful over a few things, I will make you ruler over many things. Enter into the joy of your lord.'

Jesus continued that, *"he who had received the one talent came and said, 'Lord, I knew you to be a hard man, reaping where you have not sown, and gathering where you have not scattered seed. And I was afraid, and went and hid your talent in the ground. Look, there you have what is yours.' "But his lord answered and said to him, 'You wicked and lazy servant, you knew that I reap where I have not sown, and gather where I have not scattered seed. So you ought to have deposited my money with the bankers, and at my coming I would have received back my own with interest. So take the talent from him, and give it to him who has ten talents. 'For to everyone who has, more will be given, and he will have abundance; but from him who does not have, even what he has will be taken away. And cast the unprofitable servant into the outer darkness. There will be weeping and gnashing of teeth.'*

It serves better to walk with God because of your love for Him. Jesus in John 14:15 relates what the motivation should be when on a journey with Him. He said "if you love Me, keep my commandments." Love for God should be enough reason to want to walk with God and to honour Christ through obedience. Having pointed this important truth out, the full counsel of Scripture also makes vivid of many important reasons to want to hold onto Jesus until the very end. The consequences of not finishing the race makes the fight all worth it! While the love factor stems from a deep understanding of one's need for a relationship with God, the truth of the outcome of rejecting the journey with God allows the passion to be even more stoked. There is a great reward for those who like Paul, finish the faith race. The faith race requires true revelation of Christ, it requires commitment, sometimes it requires tenacity but critically, it also requires faith and understanding that there is an eternal reward awaiting you and in the end, it will be all more than worth it. Jesus in the beginning of the chapter in **Matthew 25,** tells us another story...

He started by saying *"the kingdom of heaven shall be likened to ten virgins who took their lamps and went out to meet the bridegroom. Now five of them were wise, and five were foolish. Those who were foolish took their lamps and took no oil with them, but the wise took oil in their vessels with their lamps. But while the bridegroom was delayed, they all slumbered and slept.*

"And at midnight a cry was heard: 'Behold, the bridegroom [a]is coming; go out to meet him!' Then

all those virgins arose and trimmed their lamps. And the foolish said to the wise, 'Give us some of your oil, for our lamps are going out.' But the wise answered, saying, 'No, lest there should not be enough for us and you; but go rather to those who sell, and buy for yourselves.' And while they went to buy, the bridegroom came, and those who were ready went in with him to the wedding; and the door was shut.

Afterward the other virgins came also, saying, 'Lord, Lord, open to us!' But he answered and said, 'Assuredly, I say to you, I do not know you.' "Watch therefore, for you know neither the day nor the hour in which the Son of Man is coming.

In this story, Jesus gives another ingredient to a successful faith race and that is: VIGILANCE and READINESS. You must be vigilant; being careful and keenly observant to detect any danger that could deter you or the resources you need to complete the journey. You must also be ready and alert, to prevent being caught off guard where the devil can tap into any weakness that you may have in your life in order to use against you or to discourage you. Here, the devil's goal is to cause you to turn away from Jesus or to cause you to start complaining and murmuring. Know that you will always need the strength of the Holy Spirit to be able to continue to keep the light in you burning.

KNOW YOUR ENEMY

There are three enemies that can affect your success in your walk with God.

Every believer in this race of faith faces these same enemies. Paul, Peter, along with all the saints mentioned in Hebrews chapter 11, and even Jesus our Great Champion, faced these same enemies. In essence, one imperative thing to know is that you do have an enemy. Yes, there is a real God and a real devil too. The devil is just as real as God is. It is mind boggling to see that some believers in certain circumstances forget that there is a real devil who goes against everything that is good for them in this life and more critically, the purpose of God for their lives. As long as you belong to God, the devil will always be an adversary to you. You have an enemy that is roaring like a lion and seeking to devour (**1 Peter 5:8**) your eternal life, your blessings, your joy, the favor of God in your life, your flourishing relationships and mostly your relationship with God. Thank God that you have a savior who loves you and is more powerful than Satan. The devil comes into a person's life to kill, to steal and to destroy. But, praise God that Jesus came so that you may have life, and life even more abundantly (**John 10:10**)! The devil has many schemes and the truth is, you are the target of all his vices.

> *"And if Satan has risen up against himself, and is divided, he cannot stand, but has an end. No one can enter a strong man's house and plunder his goods, unless he first binds the strong man. And then he will plunder his house."* – **Mark 3:26-27**

Satan is indeed a strong man when you attempt to fight him on your own. But, with the power of God, he may try but he stands no chance. It takes a stronger man to overcome a strong man.

Luke's Gospel puts it like this…

> *"When a strong man, fully armed, guards his own palace, his goods are in peace. But when a stronger than he comes upon him and overcomes him, he takes from him all his armor in which he trusted, and divides his spoils."* **Luke 11:21-22**

That strong man is the devil who is against any person without the power of God. The stronger Man is the (power of) God in the believer. The ultimate reason why Satan attacks is more than your material wealth. The devil could care less about your natural possessions. Yes, he can attack those areas to hurt you, but that is not his ultimate reason for attacking you. He attacks you through various channels in order for you to ultimately give up on God and to lose your salvation. Recently in one of our church services, I taught the story of Job in a series entitled: "How to Unlimit God in Your Life". In that series, the Holy Spirit through Scripture helped us to uncover the main reason why the devil went after Job. It is very easy to assume that the devil went after job because of Job's tangible blessings. If that was the case, the devil would have left Job alone the moment Job lost all those things, but that was not the case. The only reason the devil left Job alone was because he realized Job was not prepared to give up his faith in God no matter how the devil tried. Most times the only way to get the devil to leave you alone is to send a clear message to him that you will never give up your relationship with God no matter how hard he tries. That will certainly get him to leave you alone! It is never about your tangible things. If making you a billionaire is what will cost you to lose your good fight of faith, the devil will help you to attain all the money in the world until it comes out of your ears and nose. This is the strategy he used against the "Young Rich Ruler" (**Mark 10:17-27**), the rich man in the story of Lazarus in **Luke 16:19-31**, and many others, who gave up eternal life for the sole riches of this world. They all acquired natural wealth, but missed out on eternal life.

At the same token, if making you poor is what will cause you to lose the good fight of faith, the devil will make you poor until poverty peels away your very foreskin. This is the strategy he tried to use against Job. There are examples where the devil will either try to take away riches or allow someone to receive wealth as long as it will cost them their salvation and relationship with God. Sadly, as a Pastor, it breaks my heart to even think about the possibilities of this happening to anybody, and even more so, it hurts God's heart. The only way the devil will leave you alone is when he realizes that nothing he does against you will work and you will not give in concerning your faith in God. When he realizes that you are bound to stick with God no matter what, then he will leave you alone. It wasn't until he realized that nothing he did worked against Job that he left Job alone.

We also see this behavior of his when he tempted the Lord Jesus. He tried to overcome the Second Adam with the same schemes and tricks he did against the first Adam, but little did he know that this Adam was different! This Adam was destiny bound towards the resurrection! He offered Jesus human satisfaction, natural glory and earthly riches as a replacement for the will of God for Jesus. None of those things meant much to our Lord Jesus in comparison to the weight of glory in serving the Almighty God to the very end. Victory in any battle requires knowing the enemies of your successes. **2 Corinthians 2:11,** highlights the need to not be ignorant of the schemes of the enemy. The same Scripture indicates that Satan will take advantage of you with every opportunity that you give to him. This is why you do not give him an inch of your time, an iota of your mind or any piece of your heart. Do not entertain anything that will invite him into any area of your life or space. The three enemies of your good fight of faith are your flesh, the lust of the world and Satan himself. Interestingly, the last and ultimate enemy uses the former two for his schemes. **Galatians 5:19-21,** highlights the fact that if we seek to fulfill the desires of the flesh we will not inherit the Kingdom of God. **1 Peter 5:8** says, the devil is our key adversary and **1 John 5:4, 1 John 2:16** warns us about worldliness. Remarkably, the experience of Heaven upon the Lord's second appearance is the elimination of these three enemies of our faith. Now think about this awesome revelation of Scripture concerning the blissfulness of those who overcome and obey till the end. Ultimately, we receive a new celestial body that is not made with the same particle of this current flesh (**1 Corinthians 15:51**). This new body will have new desire, new characteristics and divine attributes; this solves the weakness of the flesh problem.

"For we know that when this earthly tent we live in is taken down (that is, when we die and leave this earthly body), we will have a house in heaven, an eternal body made for us by God himself and not by human hands. ² We grow weary in our present bodies, and we long to put on our heavenly bodies like new clothing. ³ For we will put on heavenly bodies; we will not be spirits without bodies. ⁴ While we live in these earthly bodies, we groan and sigh, but it's not that we want to die and get rid of these bodies that clothe us. Rather, we want to put on our new bodies so that these dying bodies will be swallowed up by life. ⁵ God himself has prepared us for this, and as a guarantee he has given us his Holy Spirit.

⁶ So we are always confident, even though we know that as long as we live in these bodies we are not at home with the Lord. ⁷ For we live by believing and not by seeing. ⁸ Yes, we are fully confident, and we would rather be away from these earthly bodies, for then we will be at home with the Lord. ⁹ So whether we are here in this body or away from this body, our goal is to please him. [10] For we must all stand before Christ to be judged. We will each receive whatever we deserve for the good or evil we have done in this earthly body." – **2 Corinthians 5:1-19**

Additionally, the devil will be judged right into the eternal lake of fire for eternity; this solves the Satan problem.

"The devil, who deceived them, was cast into the lake of fire and brimstone where the beast and the false prophet are. And they will be tormented day and night forever and ever." – **Revelation 20:10**

And, there shall be a new earth; this in the end solves the problem of worldliness! Glory! Hallelujah!

"Now I saw a new heaven and a new earth, for the first heaven and the first earth had passed away. Also there was no more sea." – **Revelation 21:1**

Don't forget this truth… the devil is an enemy who is against God and you. He hates you because you are in a position with God that he wanted to be in. He is the source of all evil, jealousy and envy. Scripture calls him Antichrist because Christ stands for what is good and he stands for evil. He is against you because you belong to the precious Lord. When God kicked the Devil out of heaven, Heaven said, *"Woe to you who lives on the earth"* – **Revelations 12:12**. This is a reflection of how wicked he is. This is why you need to draw near to God, and desire to go deeper in Jesus Christ.

"Submit to God. Resist the devil and he will flee from you. ⁸ Draw near to God and He will draw near to you." – **James 4:7-8**

I preached a message some time ago that I entitled D.N.A. D.N.A. in that message stands for Devils Not Allowed. You have to ensure that the devil is not allowed in any vicinity of your precious life. If God kicked Satan out of His space (heaven), you need to kick him out of your life and space as well by using the power of the Name of Jesus, just like the angel Michael did in **Jude 1:9**. The devil comes into a person's life to weaken the person's faith and to bring accusation. In **Job 1:7**, God called him *Satan*, when he went to accuse Job. The Hebrew word is *Sa-tan*, which means an adversary or one who withstands or one who resists. **Revelation 12:10** calls him *"the accuser of the brethren "* he makes accusations against you to those who are in authority to promote you and before God. **Revelation 20:2** calls him *"That serpent of Old"*. It doesn't matter how many times he peels himself or disguises himself; he is still the same ol' evil and he will always be. This is why there is no path of repentance for him. He is the devil always! The word Devil means – *atrociously wicked and cruel*. **Ephesians chapter 6**, calls him *"Wicked"*. Wickedness is: When you are fully defeated and have no legs to stand on, he still sabotages your corpse and attempts to publicly shames you beyond the end. **Isaiah 27:1** calls him *"Crooked serpent"*. **John 8:44** says, he is the *"Father of Lies"*. **2 Corinthians 4:3-4** says, he is the *"god of this age"*. That means if you don't have Jesus, he is your god. **John 10:10** calls him *"killer, thief and destroyer"*, he comes to kill your relationship with God and to steal anything that is good for you in order to destroy your life. Furthermore, **Ephesians 6** also calls him, *Ruler of darkness*... that means you can't defeat him in darkness. You can only defeat him in the light. Jesus is the Light of the World (**John 8:12**). Anything that is against Christ or your own well-being attracts the devil's wickedness. Things that will cause you to be distant from God attracts him. This is why you need to be in Christ and be in pursuit of Christ at all times. Some people, even some believers don't seek God until the devil starts tormenting their life. The Devil does so many things, but His ultimate goal is to separate you from God and to destroy your life on this earth and eventually cause you to lose your salvation; but you are the only person that can allow him to do all these wicked things to you! Jesus has given you the authority in His Own Name to keep the devil out. **Mark 16:17** says *"In My Name you will cast out devils"* **Matthew 11:12** says, *"The kingdom of God suffers violence and the violence takes it by force"*. Take your walk with God very seriously. Let your relationship with the Most High God always be your top priority. This means you can't be nice to the Devil. No dialogue! No negotiation! No counseling sessions! In **Mark 1:24**, Jesus met demons and it was on, right away *"we know who you are; you holy one of God"* they will proclaim. *"What do you want from us, you Son of God."* (**Matthew 8:29**). Jesus didn't entertain the devil and neither should you. Surrender your entire life to Jesus; not just some of it or a part of it, but all of it. It's either Jesus is the Lord of your life or not Lord at all. He has given authority to all those who have given their life to Him. As a believer, you have authority in Jesus and don't hesitate to use it! Draw near to God through awesome church services, personal devotions, ceaseless prayer life and obedience to God's Word. Satan is automatically out of places where God rules!

The Scriptures are full of scenarios where God's people tell the devil where to go. In **Matthew 8:31**, Jesus sent the devils into pigs. In **Matthew 16:23**, Jesus was speaking and the devil wanted to bring his evil deeds into the conversation; *Jesus said "Get thee behind me Satan"* In paraphrasing, Jesus said, devil! This is a "DNA" environment! The best life is a "DNA" life! God has made all things possible where the devil can never use anything to prevail against you, not even your past. **Micah 7:8** says, *"Do not rejoice over me Satan; if I fall, I shall arise; when I sit in darkness, the LORD will be a light to me."*

YOU ARE NOT ALONE

In all things, you must aim to take comfort in the fact that you are not running this race alone. If you are in the midst of trials, note that there are many Believers who are also in similar trials alongside you. If you are in victory, there are many Believers who are celebrating similar victories, therefore whether in hardship or in joy, you are not alone.

> *No temptation has overtaken you except such as is common to man; but God is faithful, who will not allow you to be tempted beyond what you are able, but with the temptation will also make the way of escape, that you may be able to bear it.*
> **– 1 Corinthians 10:13**

The attribute of God's faithfulness is only evident through trials. Faithfulness is only relevant in cases where the relationship is tested. The faithfulness of God is one of His prevalent attributes. God is faithful no matter the circumstances. You are going through the testing because God knows you can handle it with the sufficient grace that He has made available for you. Keep in mind that there are troubles in this world whether a person is a Believer of Jesus Christ or not, but in your case; you have God. Scripture has foretold you that sometimes you will be persecuted because of your faith in the Truth of God's Word.

"Blessed are you when they revile and persecute you, and say all kinds of evil against you falsely for My sake. Rejoice and be exceedingly glad, for great is your reward in heaven, for so they persecuted the prophets who were before you." – **Matthew 5:11-12**

The climate in today's world makes this scripture even more important than it has ever been. Persecution is real for many around the world and in some cases, it is simply because of faith in Jesus Christ and the decision to live out your life in Christ.

"Beloved, do not think it strange concerning the fiery trial which is to try you, as though some strange thing happened to you; but rejoice to the extent that you partake of Christ's sufferings, that when His glory is revealed, you may also be glad with exceeding joy. If you are reproached for the name of Christ, blessed are you, for the Spirit of glory and of God rests upon you. On their part He is blasphemed, but on your part He is glorified. But let none of you suffer as a murderer, a thief, an evildoer, or as a busybody in other people's matters. Yet if anyone suffers as a Christian, let him not be ashamed, but let him glorify God in this matter." - *1 Peter 4:12-16*

Whether this is happening at your workplace, in your community, among your family... wherever it may be, God sees it. He is with you. He knows these days come and therefore instructed all Believers not to be alarmed when these occurrences take place. In the case of the Apostle Paul, he was directly told. It was revealed to him exactly how he was going to suffer for God. God said,

"I must show him how he must suffer for Me."
– Acts 9:16

Can you imagine God showing you all the troubles you must suffer for His name sake the moment you receive Him into your heart? Would you be able to handle it? Just pause for a moment and think about it.

Some people can't even handle a slow motion of trials, but the Apostle was foretold and gladly accepted the assignment knowing in the end it would be all worth it. This is Paul's assertion concerning what he went through for the sake of the Name of Jesus, *"For our light affliction, which is but for a moment, is working for us a far more exceeding and eternal weight of glory."* – **2 Corinthians 4:17 9**

This ought to be your revelation, your mindset, your belief, your confession and your action. Paul believed wholeheartedly that no amount of trial in the world can come close to the weight of glory of finishing the race of faith in Christ. Through it all, Paul never gave up because He believed in the eternal God more than the strength of persecution in this passing world. Jesus Himself has also promised that

"He will never leave you nor forsake you"
(Hebrews 13:5).

One incredible truth about the journey of faith is that the Master of the journey is also the Lord of all! He has promised to be with you through the divine Person of the Holy Spirit who holds the same authority as the Father and the Lord Jesus Christ! You are encouraged to stay connected to Him through prayer, the reading of God's Word, the meditation of God's Word, and the confession of the Word of God. Sometimes the greatest hindrance to the Believer's race of faith is the ancient human desire to sin. This is an aged blockage that has hindered many Believers. Many great men and women of God have had to deal with the inner struggles of this desire. It is important to know that sin is the greatest tool of the Devil to cause you to become insensitive to the Holy Spirit as well as the things of God. When sin rules over your will, it will eventually cost you the most precious blessings of life. The more sin there is in your life, the more insensitive you become to the things of God and thereby losing your passion to finish the race you so earnestly need.

> *"Behold, the LORD's hand is not shortened, that it*
> *cannot save; nor His ear heavy, that it cannot hear.*
> *But your iniquities have separated you from your*
> *God; and your sins have hidden His face from you,*
> *So that He will not hear."* **(Isaiah 59:1-2)**

Sin affects the sinner in more than few ways. The consequences of sin hurt and affect you when caught in its snare. God despised seeing His beloved Believer enduring the painful outcome of sin. The devil will use sin to steal your joy, your integrity, your peace, your important relationships, your promotions, your future ministry, your purpose and many more. I have seen people work their entire adult life and lose it all in one single act of sin orchestrated either by the devil or by their own disobedience to God's Word. God hides His face from sin because He hates what sin does to His people. He loves His children too much to look upon what sin does to them. No matter what the world, the devil or anyone else says, God will never accept sin. Look what our sins did to His beloved Son on the cross! Jesus on the cross reveals two things: 1. God hates sin that much. 2. God loves you that much. Although no one is perfect, you the Believer must seek to live a life without the seed of sin that Jesus defeated and uprooted from your life.

> *"Whoever commits sin also commits lawlessness, and sin is lawlessness. And you know that He was manifested to take away our sins, and in Him there is no sin. Whoever abides in Him does not sin. Whoever sins has neither seen Him nor known Him. Little children, let no one deceive you. He who practices righteousness is righteous, just as He is righteous. He who sins is of the devil, for the devil has sinned from the beginning. For this purpose the Son of God was manifested, that He might destroy the works of the devil. Whoever has been born of God does not sin, for His seed remains in him; and he cannot sin, because he has been born of God."* **(1 John 3:4-9)**

These Scriptures deal with the seed (habit) of sin. The seed of sin is no longer in the person who has received Jesus Christ and is now filled with the Holy Spirit. This is the reason why when the child of God sin, the Spirit of conviction sets in until there is repentance. And when there is no repentance, the voice of the Spirit is minimized according to how long the person waits to repent. Your life in Christ does not condone sin and neither does it excuse sin. This Scripture does not mean you become immune to sin, but that when sin enters into your life, the Holy Spirit works to remove that evil act right away. God, because of His great love has given you plenty of room and grace so that sin will not rule and dominate your life.

1 John 1:9 says, **"If we confess our sins, He is faithful and just to forgive us *our* sins and to cleanse us from all unrighteousness."**

You must endeavor to give no room to the devil's wicked tool of sin. If you are struggling with any weakness of sin in your life, seek God about how to be set free! Repent and purpose in your heart not have sin rule over you! God always forgives sin that is genuinely repented through the grace and mercies of Jesus Christ. Endeavor to not place yourself in conditions and environments that make it easier for Satan to tempt you in order to contaminate your progress in God through sin. There is a difference between a sinner and a believer who has sin. A sinner carries the sin of the Adamic nature in them. Their spirit is not alive to repentance towards God. When a sinner sin, they are demonstrating the cause of a true human nature that is unregenerate. When a believer sins, the Holy Spirit reminds them of their new life in Christ and thereby birthing conviction through the Holy Spirit. The Holy Spirit is the Believers' most important Helper in the course of the journey of Faith

> *"The Spirit helps in our weaknesses. For we do not know what we should pray for as we ought, but the Spirit Himself makes intercession for us with groanings which cannot be uttered. [27] Now He who searches the hearts knows what the mind of the Spirit is, because He makes intercession for the saints according to the will of God".* (**Romans 8:26-27**)

Satan cannot use sins that God has already forgiven you against you. The key issue is true repentance. True repentance takes away the power of sin against the believer. Satan cannot use a sin repented against you. True repentance also prevents a person from trampling over the grace of God and taking the good mercies of God for granted. In other words, true repentance means you are authentically sorry for sinning against the Word of God and proposing in your heart never to commit it again. We have such a remarkable and forgiving Father who loves us unconditionally and who lets go of our faults at the very moment we ask for forgiveness. God has given what I call the ministry of Judgment to Jesus Christ who also happens to be our Attorney. What a deal! Your attorney is also the Judge!

> *"My little children, these things I write to you, so that you may not sin. And if anyone sins, we have an Advocate with the Father, Jesus Christ the righteous. [2] And He Himself is the propitiation for our sins, and not for ours only but also for the whole world."* – **1 John 2:1-2**

THE GREAT CLOUD
OF WITNESSES

The entire course of faith from Adam till today has been a race where batons are being passed from one generation to the next. The race is not a sprint. It is a marathon; but more in a sense of a relay. Believers who are living in this generation are at the tail end of the race. We are at the finishing line of their entire Kingdom marathon. We are running this race for our own good and for the good of those who may come after us. Just like how those who went ahead of us gave us their journey as our example. Our personal course of the race is within a much bigger frame of God's plan. Each race sets a platform and a foundation for the next generation of Believers. That's right... God is going to use your race as a platform for your children and/or many others who will come after you. God is and will continue to use you as an example. You have the Word of God in your life because God used those in Scriptures as an example for you. Take a careful read of these Scriptures, meditate on them have the Holy Spirit reveal to you how to apply them to your specific and personal life.

"Moreover, brethren, I do not want you to be unaware that all our fathers were under the cloud, all passed through the sea, all were baptized into Moses in the cloud and in the sea, all ate the same spiritual food, and all drank the same spiritual drink. For they drank of that spiritual Rock that followed them, and that Rock was Christ. But with most of them God was not well pleased, for their bodies were scattered in the wilderness. Now these things became our examples, to the intent that we should not lust after evil things as they also lusted. And do not become idolaters as were some of them. As it is written, "The people sat down to eat and drink, and rose up to play." Nor let us commit sexual immorality, as some of them did, and in one day twenty-three thousand fell; nor let us tempt Christ, as some of them also tempted, and were destroyed by serpents; nor complain, as some of them also complained, and were destroyed by the destroyer. Now all these things happened to them as examples, and they were written for our admonition, upon whom the ends of the ages have come. Therefore let him who thinks he stands take heed lest he fall. (**1 Corinthians 10:1-12**).

Those who have gone ahead of you into eternity are your examples. When a Believer finishes the race successfully as per the grace of God, Scriptures say they become a 'cloud of witness' in a metaphoric sense, more like in a stadium, and these 'cloud of witness' cheer on the current participators as we use their example given to us through Scriptures. Take a careful read at the following Scripture (**Hebrews 12:1-2**). Give particular attention to the underlined key words:

> *"Therefore we also, since we are <u>surrounded</u> by so great a cloud of <u>witnesses</u>, let us lay aside every weight, and the sin which so easily ensnares us, and let us run with endurance <u>the race that is set before us</u>, looking unto Jesus, the author and finisher of our faith, who for the joy that was set before Him endured the cross, despising the shame, and has sat down at the right hand of the throne of God."*

Wow! The word "surrounded" depicts a massive stadium that has encircled us. The crowd is so vast that Scriptures use the term "great" to describe them. The word "great" speaks of quantity mixed with quality. The depiction is like looking at the massiveness of clouds both above and around you. These witnesses have personal experiences, testimonies and vested interest. Some scholars believe "the great cloud of witnesses" are angels because of the term "cloud" but they are not angels. The answer is right in the Book of Hebrews. These great clouds of witnesses are cheering from an experience. They know what they are cheering about. They have direct interest in your race. They too have run the same race before. Angels do not know what it feels like to run this race because they have never run it before. This race is unique to the specific creation of God. The great crowd of witnesses like you, have also been tested on every side. They overcame the same trials, the same Devil, and have experienced the same victory that you are striving for. Before the Hebrew author got to these aforementioned Scriptures, in **Chapter 12**, the author had already informed us whom some of these witnesses are in **chapter 11.** They include Abraham, Isaac, Moses, Esther, Deborah, Elijah, and so on. This is amazing! These great men and women of God finished their race and are now cheering for you. If they were able to run their race and were successful, so can you. They did it with the help of God and so can you! There is another amazing thing in **Hebrews 11**. In verse 32, the author said *"And what more shall I say? For the time would fail me...."* In other words, there are so many more. If the Book of Hebrews were being written today you would have seen many names of Believers that you knew on this earth who have passed on to glory. This also means, your name will be part of the great cloud of witnesses when you finish your race and as soon as our loving Father calls you to eternal glory. In this race, there are clouds of witnesses who are observing; they are not by-standers. The Great clouds of witnesses are involved in the race in their own exceptional way! The progression in the Book of Hebrews gets even more exciting in a remarkable proportion! **Chapter 12** and **verses 22-24** declares that one day we are going to be together. Scripture states,

> *"But you have come to Mount Zion and to the city of the living God, the heavenly Jerusalem, to an innumerable company of angels, to the general assembly and church of the firstborn who are registered in heaven, to God the Judge of all, to the spirits of just men made perfect, to Jesus the Mediator of the new covenant, and to the blood of sprinkling that speaks better things than that of Abel."*

The great clouds of witnesses were tested on every side like you are. Again, angels have not run this race before. **Hebrews chapter 12** is a continuation of **Hebrews chapter 11**, and tells us that these great people of faith are now with the Lord, as witnesses of our current race here on earth. Other scholars have also suggested that the crowd of witnesses are only the saints of the Old Testament due to the fact that no New Testament Believer was named. This assertion is also inaccurate. There were no New Testament Believers mentioned because there was no New Testament at that particular time in terms of canonization. During the times of the Apostles, the New Testament saints were the living Scriptures of the time in bodily form. Their lives are our Scriptures in this era and dispensation, just like how the lives of the Old Testament saints were their Scriptures in their time on this earth. We who now are alive have the grace of having both the saints of the Old Testament and the New Testament to learn from as our examples. The Hebrew author could not have added those that are in the New Testament because they were mere contemporaries to the author. But to us who are alive today, the likes of Paul, Peter, James, John, Timothy and so on, are our heroes of Scripture along with the Old Testament saints. They ran their race and they did it in a pleasing way to the Lord. **Hebrews 11:32**, tells us that there were more names, but time will fail for the mentioning of all. Paul in **2 Tim. 4:7** said,

> *"I have fought the good fight, I have finished the race, I have kept the faith, finally, there is laid up for me the crown of righteousness."*

Today, that Hall of Faith includes Paul and all who will pass on to the Lord into eternity from the beginning of time until today. It will one day include you and myself when our gracious and merciful Lord cease to tarry. If you have a loved one who has passed on in the faith – they're watching. They are cheering you on! They are saying, "you can do it"! They are saying, "do not give up", they are urging you on, they are proclaiming... "use our example". There are many of them. They are saying "look we did it and you will do it too". The word "Great" is not in reference to power or authority but "Great" as in numeration. Our authority and greatness are in the Holy Spirit and not in the "cloud" (numbers). Here, "Great cloud" means there are many who are cheering you on with their testimony of how gracious and merciful God was to them on this earth, and that same gracious and merciful God will continue to help you to the end. The Apostle John through Jesus' own words shows us that those who have passed on into glory, see what happens with those who are still on this earth. In **John 8:56** the Lord Jesus said,

> *"Your father Abraham rejoiced to see My day, and*
> *he saw it and was glad."*

Jesus said Abraham had longed for the fulfilment of the promise that was given to him by God (**Genesis 22:18**). That promise was to be fulfilled through the life of Christ on this earth (**Galatians 3:16**). Abraham who had died over thousands of years before Jesus' life and death on this earth saw it and he (Abraham) was glad. The promise that Abraham was looking forward to was the promise of the "Seed". Many have believed that the promise of "Seed" to Abraham in **Genesis 22:18** was a promise of Isaac to Abraham but that's not the case. Isaac was the initiation of many channels to the actual Seed. Remember, Jesus' life that was to be manifested on this earth was first described as Seed in Scriptures (**Genesis 3:15**). That was the same term God used in Abraham's event. God Himself called Jesus "Seed" in the book of Genesis. Isaac was a channel just like Jacob, and then Judah, and eventually through David and then finally the actual Seed, which is Jesus Christ. God never said to Abraham that Isaac was the Seed. As a matter of truth, God said to *Abraham "In Isaac your Seed shall be called"* in other words, your Seed shall be called out of Isaac.

> **Galatians 3:19** says the law was given to the Israelites *"until the <u>Seed should come to whom the promise was made; and it was appointed through angels by the hand of a mediator."</u>* This proves that Israel was to still wait for the promised Seed even through the times of the giving of the law through Moses (**John 1:17**).

> **Galatian 3:16** definitely states, *"Now to Abraham and his Seed were the promises made. He does not say, "And to seeds," as of many, but as of one, "And to your Seed," who is Christ."*

This is why Abraham longed to see the days of Christ on this earth. The manifestation of Christ is the true fulfilment of the promise made by God to Abraham. Through Christ, Abraham was officially made the Father of many nations because only Christ can bring many nations to God in order for Abraham to become the father of the faith as one who first believed God for righteousness (**Genesis 15:6; Romans 4:3; Genesis 3:6**). Unlike those who lived under the law in the Old Testament, Abraham lived by Faith. Isaac, Jacob, eventually Moses, etc., all lived by the promise and covenant made between God and Abraham. Therefore, Abraham was exceptionally glad to see the life of Christ. These great groups of Believers are watching you as you run your race. They are not in haste to see you finish as they are more interested in your finishing no matter how much time your race may take. They too understand that they finished their race with different duration. Remember that the Kingdom of God is not a Sprint. It is more like a relay within a Marathon. A 'baton' has been passed on from those that have gone on ahead of you. You must run the race. You must do your part with diligence and endurance like they did. They are cheering you on because some of them gave their lives so that you do not have to give yours like they did. Some of them gave up everything so that you can have the Word of God in your hand; so that you will have the whole story and the whole counsel of God. So that you will have someone who also runs the same race to look up to, to inspire you and to finally cheer you on. They are cheering you on because they believe that their race is incomplete without your race in this relay. They know that you have a better and more complete message than they had. They cheer because we are on the same team as them against the devil and his wishes of hell for you. They want you to be successful in completing what they started. Even our Lord Jesus ran the race too. Again,

"Therefore we also, since we are surrounded by so great a cloud of witnesses, let us lay aside every weight, and the sin which so easily ensnares us, and let us run with endurance the race that is set before us, ² looking unto Jesus, the [a]author and [b] finisher of our faith, who for the joy that was set before Him endured the cross, despising the shame, and has sat down at the right hand of the throne of God." **Hebrews 12:1-2**

WEIGHT THAT BESETS

Within every generation or era – there has always been weights that carry the potential of besetting the participants of the race. In the time of Adam, it was the first temptation of the devil! And then we have Noah, Abraham, Lot, Esther, Moses, the Early Church, etc. The Word of God cautions us today to *"lay aside every weight, and the sin which so easily besets us"*

The issue of sin is formally addressed. The weight and sin are two different things – Sin is disobedience to God's Word and thereby missing the mark. The "weights" are unnecessary strings that have the potential ability to pull you back from pressing on or delaying your advancement. For example: The modern day pressure from the spirit of anti-Christ is called a weight. Anger is a weight. Lusts, laziness, unwilling to progress, selfishness, are all weight. It is important to cut these weights off and run with endurance in the race that is set before you. No "weight" is worth losing your faith or salvation over! Although we are called to occupy and work in the Kingdom until "that day" (**2 Timothy 1:12**), the word of God does not want you to forget that when it is all set and done; you are sojourners who are on a pilgrimage. Cut off anything that will try to discourage you; or make the race difficult. Anything that will try to make you quit as you pursue the ultimate and glorious prize!

There are two variables that support us in an encouraging way in this race:

1. "Looking unto Jesus, the author and the finisher of our faith"

   ▪ Jesus is our Master Encourager (with the works of death, burial and resurrection, along with His Word, and his example of endurance, He has given you everything that you need to be victorious coupled with showing you the way through His life on the earth and through His Word.

2. And then you have the great cloud of witnesses:

   ▪ They support with cheers and testimonies of God's faithfulness
   ▪ We can study their lives and see the power of God's faithfulness, and also learn from their success and from their mistakes.

It is always good in every endeavor to keep something ahead of you that motivates you. In the Kingdom of God, it is the facts of our glorious and ultimate destination along with the faithful testimonies of the crowd of witnesses. Clement of Alexandria (Early church leader) described the "great cloud of witnesses" as "a numberless multitude above us, like a cloud, 'holy and glorified.'

"They are cheering, as the crowd of spectators give additional motivation to the combatants, so the cloud of witnesses who have themselves been in the same contest, ought to increase our earnestness." Clement continued.

Some lost their lives in order to make the race, others gave up their livelihoods, others were abandoned by their families, some lost their homes, so on, but in the end, they made it to eternal glory. To them, even if they lived to be 120 years old on this earth, that life is only a tiny dot in comparison to a blissful eternal life. They lived on this earth for an eternal cause, not just for themselves but also for the next generation. Every time you read about a hero or a heroine in the Scriptures, their story and life is cheering you on. The Hebrew author tells us that even Jesus ran this race. He went through the hardship in the days of his flesh on this earth.

> Jesus, *"who, in the days of His flesh, when He had offered up prayers and supplications, with vehement cries and tears to Him who was able to save Him from death, and was heard because of His godly fear, though He was a Son, yet He learned obedience by the things which He suffered.* ⁹ *And having been perfected, He became the author of eternal salvation to all who obey Him"* **(Hebrew 5:8-9)**

That is why you can look to Him. He is not just our example, He is our perfect example. An example of how to trust in God and how to rely on the Holy Spirit (**Luke 4:1**). He went through what you are going through and even worse to be precise...

"For in that He Himself has suffered, being
tempted, He is able to aid those who are tempted"
– **Hebrews 2:8**

Jesus did the hardest of the work for you. Most of the Old Testament men and women of God had it more difficult than us. Think of Stephen who gave his life and died slowly by the scourging pain of rough stones being heaved at him. In every adventure, the beginning and the foundation is always the most difficult. They had it worse, and if they made it, so will we. Even today, there are many Believers who are severely being persecuted simply because they have received the same revelation as you, and professes Christ as their Lord and Savior. Be inspired! Be motivated! Press on! While God is still giving you the grace of life on this earth, live your life wisely by making every day count. In Luke's account of the parable of the talent, the Master told the servants who had received the talents to *"occupy this He come"* in the King James Version. (**Luke 19:13**). The New King James translation says *"Do (Kingdom) business till I come"*. While on this earth, God has mandated your life with the business of the Kingdom. You must redeem the time.

You do that by helping build the Kingdom. Be a minister (serve) at your local church. Help the Pastor to win souls and to touch lives with the message of the Kingdom. Witness to others about Christ, share your testimonies, tell others about what Christ has done for you, help the needy and tell them Jesus sent you to bless them. Declare Christ to your friends and neighbours. Touch those who are being oppressed by the devil. Encourage others. Pray for those who are suffering. Be a financier of the gospel. Take on your role as minister of reconciliation.

It is paramount to have Kingdom mentality, because we are Kingdom bound:

- Let us set our eyes on Jesus, the King of the Kingdom – and all that He has done for us!
- Let us serve God with all our hearts, let's give Him our all.
- We are in to win this thing!

His appearance is so close that He could come anytime. We are looking forward to Him coming back but until then we have: Souls to save, purpose to fulfill, destinies to embrace, work to do and His church to be built! God has given us the Ministry gifts (**Ephesians 4:11**-16) to build you up in order to get you there. At the finishing line is a crown, rewards, new body, joy, peace, blissfulness, and many more but most importantly, Jesus will be there for eternity! Until then, we must impact our generation... we must put a watermark on this generation! Jesus overcame because He kept His eyes on the prize – He saw your salvation as greater reward than the challenges during the days of His flesh on this earth – *"Now looking unto Jesus, the author and finisher of our faith, who for the joy that was set before Him endured the cross, despising the shame"* (**Hebrews 12:2**).

It is a voyage – a pilgrimage:

- We are the sojourners / pilgrims
- There will be a big party once we all arrive.

When you get there, which is the ultimate destination of Mount Zion, the City of the living God and the heavenly Jerusalem... there will be:

- An innumerable company of angels awaiting you.
- The general assembly of the universal saints will be there.
- The Church of the firstborn who are registered in heaven,
- God the Judge of all will be there.
- The spirits of just men made perfect (Abraham, etc., and loved ones who have gone ahead.
- At that place is, Jesus the Mediator of the new covenant, and to the blood of sprinkling that speaks better things than that of Abel

God saved the best for last:

- We are building on the foundation of Christ.
- We are living in the wonderful outpouring of the Spirit of God.
- This is the greatest time to be born-again and to serve the Lord; it is the best time to be a Believer of Jesus Christ. There are greater things awaiting us in eternity.

You must long to hear these amazing words from the Lord Jesus Christ, *"well done my good and faithful servant"*. No matter what comes your way, these words from Jesus make your journey of faith worthwhile and worth all the troubles. To hear such endearing words from the King of kings and the Lord of lords. To receive such kind and receptive words from Calvary's victor, the One who made it all possible. To hear such incredible words from the One who made it all and yet gave it all for you. To hear Him affirm that you too have passed the test of life on this earth. You ran the race and just like the Believer of Scripture, you too shall receive a crown. This truth makes all the trials, the tribulations, the endurance, the snares, all worth it. There is no circumstance or adversity that isn't worth the awaiting glory.

2 Corinthians 4:17, *"for our light affliction, which is but for a moment, is working for us a far more exceeding and eternal weight of glory"*

The afflictions are not eternal. You cannot allow a temporal affliction to rob you of God's eternal glory. Never allow the affliction to get to you or into you. If you allow it to get into you, it will generate discontentment and discouragement, which holds the potential of stealing your joy and stymying your faith. Guard your heart. Jesus said, *"the ruler of this world is coming, and he has nothing in Me"* Jesus did not commit Himself to the devil no matter what the devil tried to do against His purpose and the Father's will for His life. He said the devil 'holds nothing over Me'. In other words, He said, there is nothing the devil can do that will cause me to yield to his tricks. Jesus was so confident in His faith in the Father. He had made up His mind that He was going with God all the way. This is the kind of faith you need to aspire to. Jesus is truly your perfect example. He placed His journey with the Father on this earth above all else. What great examples for us!

THE FALL AWAY

In this relay (within a marathon) race, different outcomes occur with respective participants due to diverse trials and unique experiences. Some will fall away, others will give up, but there are those who will be determined to cross the finishing line. You must purpose in your heart that the latter will be you! You must know that it will surely be worth your while to overcome. Paul warned the church about the fall away so that you will not be surprised when you witness the occurrences.

> *"Let no one deceive you by any means; for that Day will not come unless the falling away comes first."*
> **2 Thessalonians 2:3.**

The aforementioned Scripture is a warning to all Believers. The spirit of anti-Christ will be so enraged by his pending final demise that he will do all he can to divert you from your divine destination and eternal reward. In the Apostle's letter to Timothy, his son in the faith, he warned Believers of the schemes of the devil. He said,

> *"Now the Spirit expressly says that in latter times some will depart from the faith, giving heed to deceiving spirits and doctrines of demons, speaking lies in hypocrisy, having their own conscience seared with a hot iron."* – **1 Timothy 4:1-2.**

The devil isn't too excited about your relationship with God, your future and your eternal life. He does not want to go to his final destination, which is the eternal lake of fire with his fallen angels alone. He wants revenge on you - God's favoured creation. He wants revenge against God. He knows the only way to hurt the heart of God is to hurt you and to deviate you from God's glorious plans for you. When you are faced with these darts and schemes of the enemy, will you fail Jesus? Will you deny Him? Would you refute His Church? Would you reject His infallible Word? Would you refuse the Truth? Would you oppose His Spirit? Would you turn down your own eternal salvation? Or, will you finish the race? **Revelation 12:12** says, 'when the devil realizes that his end is at hand, he will throw everything at you.' The Holy Spirit through Scripture foretold you so that when the time comes, you will not be dismayed. Your task at hand is to be strong, to be courageous and to be unmovable. Quite often I see people who once were on fire for God. They had tasted the heavenly calling. They eat of the table of God's Word, and then something unexpected happens to them or in the selected view of God and then all of a sudden they give up to the lies and the pressures of the devil. They give in to the schemes of the devil and to the pleasures of this world. There will be times when nothing you possess in the natural will be enough to save you. When you are faced with those times, never forget that you have the Holy Spirit in you, and that this world is only temporal. Be vigilant, be alert, and be careful not to follow those who cultivate and walk in antichrist spirit. Be watchful not to be deceived by the schemes of the world or the deceptions of the ways of this passing world.

YOU ARE OF CHRIST

For all intents and purposes, no one ever starts a race without the desire to want to finish the race. It is the unexpected bump in the road that catches the participants off guard at times. It is imperative to keep in mind that no other offers can make up for what God has in-store of you. Before you can gather the surge of finishing the race you must first perceive that you are not of this world. The world has nothing better to offer that can exceed the eternal bliss of the glorious reward of living for Christ, coupled with the much better way of life on this earth. Even above the ultimate gift of eternal life, a life with Christ on this earth is simply worth it. Just because you have life on this earth does not mean that you originated from this earth. As a born again Believer, your obedience to the World of God saves you from many temptations and trials. There are deep and there are simple benefits to being an obedient follower of Jesus. With the help of the Spirit, the Word of God in your life will prevent you from serious and destructive behaviors and habits that can destroy your life even before the day of judgement. My wife and I have this act of using an idea as one of the excuses we give ourselves to enjoy our marriage even more. We know that because of Christ, we choose to not drink alcohol nor take any destructive drugs. Earlier in our marriage, we will save up money that we may have had to spend if we had those unhealthy habits. We will be so thankful to the Lord for it and use the money for other means; including spicing up our relationship with Friday night evening dinners. We will humorously call it our "drug money" or "alcohol money". Most of my daily prayer times are spent by thanking God from what the simple obedience of His Word continues to deliver me from. The obedience to the Word of God inspires a person from breaking the law of the land, it prevents adultery, and it prevents sexually transmitted diseases that come by way of fornications and sexual promiscuity. These are just a few of the many things that the power of God's word saves a person from. Your new birth in the Spirit gave you a new life of the Spirit. When you become born again, the core and the root of your new life is God. You are of God. God gave birth to you by His Spirit. Your first birth was of the flesh with sinful Adamic nature. Your first birth could not produce the necessities for a relationship with God. You were of the flesh but God is Spirit. In order for you to have the life of Christ, you had to be born again. God had to give you the grace to experience what it is like to be led by His Spirit, so He gave you a rebirth experience not with human nature but with the very nature of God. This is why God not only loves you but he also made you His offspring. Being God's offspring means God has willingly taken on the responsibility of your wellbeing on this earth. He has great interest in your purpose and in your wellbeing. He has begun a great work in you, and He will ensure to complete it as long as you continue to trust Him and not give up. He will not leave you as long as you are determined and purposed in your heart to follow Him. God has willfully accepted the full role to provide, preserve and to protect you. Your walk in Jesus Christ demands that you stay focused, not on this earth but in your eternal destination, which is heaven.

"Set your mind on this above" (**Colossians 3:2**).

The Disciples were called into glory and eternity through various hardship and remarkable means. The truth is, as a true Believer of Christ, it does not matter when and how you are called. However, whenever you are called, you just want to be ready. You must walk in the wisdom of God. Be wise on this earth, your primary navigation is towards heaven.

"Store up treasure in heaven…." (**Matthew 6:19-20**).

You are a pilgrim and a sojourner (**1 Peter 2:11**). This world is not your home, you are just passing through. God will continue to watch over you, and most importantly, He is leading you to an eternal blessing. You have a promise of the life which now is and the one to come (**1 Timothy 4:8**). Your foremost effort and goal are to finish the race like the Lord Jesus did. Like Paul, Mary the mother of our Lord, Joana, Esther, Peter, Elijah, and the rest did. It is awesome to be named amongst these great men and women who have also walked on the face of this earth like you are. With all the extreme measures and pressures, Paul yet kept on because he knew what He was after was more important than the pressures around Him. He kept himself inspired by the fact that the purpose has more value than the hardship of the process. He said, due to that revelation, he kept on pressing forward. As you navigate the corridors of life towards your God-given purpose, it is highly important to keep the end results as a motivation. One of the greatest strategies that God used in leading Israel from Egypt into the promised land was a constant reminder of the great outcome of arriving at the land flowing with milk and honey. When Israel would become weary, he would remind them that the trip was worth it, and that every step forward is a step further away from bondage and a step closer to their desired destination. Each day that passes by in your life as you continue to do what it takes to fulfill your purpose is a step closer to fulfilling your purpose.

He said, *"Brethren, I do not count myself to have [d]apprehended; but one thing I do, forgetting those things which are behind and reaching forward to those things which are ahead, [14] I press toward the goal for the prize of the upward call of God in Christ Jesus."* **Philippians 3:13-14**

You understand the steps towards your final redemption.

"In Him you also *trusted,* after you heard the word of truth, the gospel of your salvation; in whom also, having believed, you were sealed with the Holy Spirit of promise, [14] who is the [e]guarantee of our inheritance until the redemption of the purchased possession, to the praise of His glory." Ephesians 1:13-14

Ephesians 1:13-14 explains that although you are saved, you are still waiting for a final redemption. This is a powerful message that reveals the depth of your walk with Jesus Christ. Your walk with Christ is a divine journey, and a process at that. The first step of this journey and process is becoming born again. It is quite incredible the natural process of life on this earth parallels the journey of faith in Jesus Christ. Before anyone comes into this world they must be born naturally. Every human being is born as a baby first. The usual initial food of nutrition is soft food, usually something of a milky texture. In moments the baby begins to make use of their eyes to see; they then go through a process of discerning, learning, standing, talking, walking, etc. Likewise, the initial process of your walk with God is to be born again. Scripture teaches about standing in the faith, walking spiritually, seeing spiritually, using Kingdom language, discerning, etc. These are all important phases and components of your need in order to finish your race and finish well. You as the believer of Christ have a duty to learn and to grow through these stages. Knowing where you are in these stages and yearning to excel into the next level of your walk is an absolute necessity. Let us discuss the first phase of being born again and what that means.

THE PROCESS

One of the most important revelations to have within the process of your journey is knowing the importance of the elements of the faith that God has established for the flourishing of your relationship with Him. The closer you are to God, the stronger you are in Him. *"Draw near to God and He will draw near to you...."* (**James 4:8**). Committed adherence to Scripture, Prayer, Worship, and continual fasting are the only ingredients given to you in order for you to draw near to God. Drawing near to God means you are governed and covered by His divine principles and protected by His supernatural strength. Just like how your body needs nutrition from food, and water, so that your spirit needs nutrition from these divinely given elements of the faith. Quite often Believers will find themselves giving more attention to their natural life more than their spiritual, and although it is important to feed your natural body well and to exercise, the benefit is greater in comparison to being fit in the Spiritual.

"Bodily exercise profits a little, but godliness is profitable for all things, having promise of the life that now is and of that which is to come." – **1 Timothy 4:8**

Physical nourishment can only profit on this earth but much effort into your spiritual life profits both your life on this earth and for eternity.

> *"And I, brethren, could not speak to you as to spiritual people but as to carnal, as to babes in Christ. ² I fed you with milk and not with solid food; for until now you were not able to receive it, and even now you are still not able."* – **1 Corinthians 3:1-2**

Being a babe in Christ is equated to having worldly cravings and struggling with fully understanding the depth of the Kingdom of God. This is nothing to be ashamed of if you are a new believer. However, there is an expectation for growth as you spend more time walking with God. There is an obvious frustration in the tone of Paul's description of the "babes" in Christ. This comes with the length of time they had been in Christ and yet not progressing to higher maturation. Spiritual maturity does not always correlate with a person's duration of time in the Church. Spiritual maturity is according to a person's hunger… a person's passion for the Lord, their teachable spirit, and the willingness to fully yield to the Spirit of Christ and obedience to God's Word. A person can sit in the church chairs for 35 years, but may never reach the extent of a person who has only been in the Kingdom for 20 months with the quality of hunger required to grow. Divine wisdom says, *"…those who seek me shall find me"* (**Proverbs 8:17**). Jesus said, *"Blessed are those who hunger after righteousness for they shall be filled"* (**Matthew 5:6**).

"As newborn babes, desire the pure milk of the word, that you may grow" – **1 Peter 2:2**

The state of being an infant in the Spirit refers to the moment you receive Christ as the Lord over your life. There are exciting aspects of babies and not so flattering aspects of babies.

The awesome part of being a baby is the joy of the family in receiving the child. Jesus said, the heavens rejoice when a soul comes to Christ. The Kingdom of God rejoices over the birth of a soul into the glorious Kingdom of God. Your natural life is like a type of your spiritual walk. When you become born again, you are immediately a "new born baby" in Christ. There are aspects of Scripture that the Word identifies as basic or elementary. These are the first things to know. There are also some aspects of Scripture that are meant for those who are mature. Again, maturity does not necessarily mean duration of time in the Kingdom of God. A person can be saved for many years and still be immature. Age is never a factor when it comes to maturity. For example, evidence of maturity in Christ includes appreciation of God's Word, obedience, tithing, being a blessing to others, etc. The baby in the household takes, but the parents give. You know you are mature when your life begins to be a blessing to others in the Kingdom of God. When a person is in the baby phase, you give them milk, and they only take.

NUTRITION

"Therefore, leaving the discussion of the elementary
principles of Christ, let us go on to [a]perfection, not
laying again the foundation of repentance from dead
works and of faith toward God, ²of the doctrine of
baptisms, of laying on of hands, of resurrection of the
dead, and of eternal judgment." – **Hebrews 6:1-2**

In the Gospel of John; the fourth chapter, the disciples were
urging Jesus to eat physical food. Jesus revealed to them that he
had eaten spiritual food.

In **verse 34** He said, *"My meat is to do the will of*
Him who sent Me, and to finish His work."

The Greek Word used by Jesus Christ in **John 4:34** is *"Broma"*,
which is directly translated "meat". Here, Jesus referred to certain
aspects of the spiritual phase and element as meat. There is a
level in God that requires the Believer to drink milk and there
are other levels that when the Believer gets to, he or she is able
to take in meat. Meat is solid food and milk is soft food. Milk

is for babes and meat is for the mature. If you give a baby meat, they may choke on it. Some good solid food does not interest a child because they lack the knowledge or the understanding regarding how precious that meat is. I have seen many immature Believers undermine a powerful revelation or even fall asleep under a powerful and deep teaching due to lack of appreciation and understanding. May the Lord increase your passion and desire for Him in Jesus Name as you navigate the race of faith, may you develop stronger sensitivity for the elements of the faith and for the things of God. May you continue to grow into full maturity through the ingredients of the faith in Jesus Name!

> *"For though by this time you ought to be teachers, you need someone to teach you again the first principles of the oracles of God; and you have come to need milk and not solid food. For everyone who partakes only of milk is unskilled in the word of righteousness, for he is a babe. But solid food belongs to those who are of full age, that is, those who by reason of use have their senses exercised to discern both good and evil."* - **Hebrews 5:12-14**

The matured in Christ can handle tough circumstances. They are trained to train others (***"For though by this time you ought to be teachers"***). The matured do not only receive, they also give. In a household, children take but the mature give. A young and immature tree doesn't yield fruits, in other words it cannot give. Matured trees give... it gives fruits. This is how you can measure whether you are matured or still have some growing to do. A matured Believer knows that they are not saved just to go to heaven but to also carry on the ministry of reconciliation (**2 Corinthians 5:18**) until their race is completed here on this earth, and until they go to eternal glory. The matured Believer is not easily swayed by every wind of doctrine. This is God's desire for you, that you will be nurtured into maturity until the coming of the Lord. **Ephesians 4:12-14** urges that this is the main reason why God has given the ministry of the five-fold gifts to the church, *"for the equipping of the saints for the work of ministry, for the [e]edifying of the body of Christ, ¹³ till we all come to the unity of the faith and of the knowledge of the Son of God, to a perfect man, to the measure of the stature of the fullness of Christ; ¹⁴ that we should no longer be children, tossed to and fro and carried about with every wind of doctrine, by the trickery of men, in the cunning craftiness of deceitful plotting."*

There is a progressive expectation that comes with your journey with God. The more you grow, the easier you are able to take on the darts of the enemy. The matured is not easily tossed to and fro from every wind of doctrine.

SEEING

The next phase of your walk with God is the grace to see things the way God meant for you to see. It is called having "spiritual eyes". There is a massive difference between having natural eyes and having spiritual eyes. The natural eyes give aid to seeing the natural but you see things in the spirit and with the understanding of God when you have spiritual eyes. One of the initial stages of a child is to develop the skill to see. Seeing helps you to identify people and objects once you gain the skills to see as an infant. You begin to recognize your loved ones by seeing their faces repeatedly.

> *"Therefore, from now on, we regard no one according to the flesh. Even though we have known Christ according to the flesh, yet now we know Him thus no longer." 2 Corinthians 5:15*

In the Kingdom of God, you are to know no one after the flesh but after the spirit. In the first Chapter of the Gospel of Luke, Scripture says,

"Now Mary arose in those days and went into the hill country with haste, to a city of Judah, and entered the house of Zacharias and greeted Elizabeth. And it happened, when Elizabeth heard the greeting of Mary, that the babe leaped in her womb; and Elizabeth was filled with the Holy Spirit." (Verses 39-41)

Even though both the Lord Jesus and John the Baptist were in the mother's womb respectively, they knew each other before they were manifested in the flesh. This is what it means when God says *"I knew you before you were in your mother's womb"* (**Jeremiah 1:5**). Those with spiritual eyes discern by way of the Spirit and not by the flesh. God knew you before you were ever a thought on this earth. You are known in the Spirit first before the natural. God made the natural to be so through imitation of the supernatural. Jesus in His conversation with Nicodemus in John chapter 3 asserted that if Nicodemus could not perceive the things of the spirit through illustrations by the natural means, how can he understand the things of the spirit. Natural things are the natural manifestation of how things operate in the Spirit first. This is why Jesus will always use parables with natural people and natural instances to show the Kingdom of God. Natural order, food for nutrition, communications, inventions, social contract, laws, etc., are all examples of how things work in the Spirit. You can understand how things work in the Spirit by bringing the illustration of how they work in the natural. This is the advantage that the people of the Spirit have. We know it first before it is manifested in the natural. **Hebrews 11:3** says the Spirit is the mother of the visible things that we now see. It is one thing to have eyes to see natural things, but it is a whole different thing to have eyes in the spirit. Jesus in the Gospels (**Matthew 13:13**; **Mark 8:18**) said he spoke in parables so that *"having (natural) eyes they may not see (in the Spirit) and having (natural) ears they may not perceive (things of the Spirit)."* Jesus is disclosing the wonderful insight that there is a difference between having natural eyes and having spiritual eyes. Natural eyes see natural things, but spiritual eyes see the things of God and therefore are more important. A person with spiritual eyes sees more and understands more than a person with just natural eyes. One of the initial stages of your walk with God is your ability to begin to see with your spiritual eyes in order to discern spiritual things. Just like the natural eyes, your spiritual eyes can be improved or can go dimmer. You can also have spiritual eyes but lose it eventually if you do not sharpen it with the ingredients and the matters of the faith. There are many in the church today who are blind. They do not see where the church is in the Scriptural timeline of God, and neither do they understand this present events and how they relate to the church. Some can only partially see. You can sharpen your spiritual eyes by seeking the Truth of God through His Word and by being an active partaker of the heavily calling here on earth. This desire and action will enhance your spirit sight. In addition, you must pray for understanding and for a deeper spiritual sight. This is obtained by your action and passion toward God and the things of God. **1 John 2:11** tells us that spiritual darkness can blind a person's spiritual eyes. As in the natural, when the eyes remain in darkness for too long, it can affect the eyes negatively. In the same way, when a person becomes accustomed to sin and the evil mindset of this dark world, it will affect their spiritual sight. When a person distances themselves from prayer, from the reading and the meditation of the Word of God, gathering of the saints, and becomes disobedient to the voice of the Spirit, it will surely affect their spiritual sight in a negative way.

In **Ephesians 1:18**, the Apostle Paul prayed that *"the eyes of your understanding being enlightened; that you may know what is the hope of His calling, what are the riches of the glory of His inheritance in the saints."*

When you have spiritual eyes, you become enlightened to the glorious things of the Spirit. You see what God is doing on this earth and with His church. You see the evil works of the devil and you are able to thwart and oppose it successfully. The Apostle highlighted, **"by now you ought to be teachers."** A person who is spiritually blind cannot and should not lead the people of God. How can the blind lead the blind lest they both fall into a ditch (**Matthew 15:14**). Spiritual eyes give you the ability to see Scripture as God intended His Word to be perceived. When your spiritual eyes are enlightened, you see what God is doing more than what the devil is trying to do. One of the greatest ways to overcome wickedness and darkness is having the light of the Word shine upon you. Without spiritual sight, people become backbiters and complainers and are in most cases against what God is doing in and with His own Church. They will mummer too often against the leading of the Spirit through the Pastor. With spiritual sight, they become helpers of the harvest. They see what God is doing and are gladly involved. They become teachers and exemplars to the less matured. They see the works and the intentions of the devil. This is how Job overcame the vile temptation of Satan in Satan's attempt to derail him from his spiritual position in God. Job said *"His lamp shone upon my head, and when by His light I walked through darkness"* (**Job 29:3**). Job overcame the trap of the Devil because God's candle over him allowed him to see through the darkness of Satan. May the Lord cause His candle to shine upon your head. May you receive a powerful and enlightened spirit eyes to see in the Spirit in Jesus Name!

HEARING

In most cases when I am dealing with a situation involving tough decisions, I often pray and wait on the Lord to grant me His wonderful and merciful grace to hear His voice through His Word and by His Spirit over and above all other voices. Sometimes in a sincere effort to receive counsel, a person could say what seems like the right thing to you but the intention may not be of God. An incredible example is seen in the Gospel of **John chapter 12**, when Mary of Bethany desired to anoint the feet of Jesus with the expensive oil. The Scriptures actually say,

> *"Mary took a pound of very costly oil of spikenard, anointed the feet of Jesus, and wiped His feet with her hair".*

Now, you have to imagine how expensive this oil was. In those days, costly oil or perfume was not factory made like the ones you have today. The oil that Mary of Bethany used was quite scarce and therefore very short in supply. They were handmade and only the rich would have it. The gesture by Mary to the Saviour and Teacher was an extreme demonstration of appreciation for Jesus.

The action was not just a mere anointing. Mary seemed to have spent quite a fortune for this precious oil. In **verse 7** Jesus said that the anointing of His feet was actually a preparation for His impending burial. Now comes Judas of all people, who seemingly "cares more about the plight of the poor, than Jesus the most gracious of all".

Judas suggested that Mary of Bethany be stopped, and for the precious and expensive oil be sold in order to be given to the poor. Now what a kind gesture it appeared, by the one who will eventually betray the Messiah. Jesus' response was a direct rebuke to what Judas was seemingly attempting, as he tried to make it look like he cared for the poor more than anyone else present.

Thank God that Jesus hears beyond what human words utter. Sometimes religious people can say the right things to derail visions and the will of God. A statement like Judas' assertion puts a person in a very difficult situation. On one hand you do not want to seem like wasting resources and ignoring the poor, and on the other hand you know the resources are meant for God-given purpose. If you use the resources for the latter, you run the risk of being accused of not caring for the poor and on the contrary, if you use it for the former you are outside of the purpose of God. Judas' statement put Jesus at a junction of making it seem as though He does not care for the poor when most of Jesus' ministry was rooted in doing just that, caring for the vulnerable. Thank God for the grace of hearing with spiritual ears. May the Lord grant you the grace to hear beyond human words. One of the powerful tools to have in your walk of faith is the ability to hear from the Word of God and by the Spirit. Jesus rebuked spiritual deafness in His ministry here on earth. A person who is spiritually deaf should not lead those who want to hear from God. It is impossible to hear what God is saying to the churches if the supposed hearer cannot hear anything from God. When your ability to hear is restricted to natural hearing you will never find the things of God fascinating or as a necessity as you should or as needed.

Jesus quoted Isaiah's prophetic utterance by saying *"And in them the prophecy of Isaiah is fulfilled, which says: 'Hearing you will hear and shall not understand, and seeing you will see and not perceive; for the hearts of this people have grown dull. Their ears are hard of hearing, And their eyes they have closed, lest they should see with their eyes and hear with their ears, lest they should understand with their hearts and turn, so that I should heal them.'*

It is key to desire and to receive these spiritual senses in your walk with God. If you don't have these spiritual senses, pray to God, pursue, pay attention, be sensitive to the Spirit and most of all, be hungry for these ingredients of the faith.

TALKING

Talking is the most important medium of communication. Scripture uses words like, decree, declare, words, confess, and speech as medium of communication. Salvation comes by confessions. Blessings are proclaimed by decreeing and declaring. Forgiveness takes place through confessing (and repenting).

In **Psalm 19**, Scriptures say creation uttered speech to declare the glory of God. Words are used in the Kingdom of God to create, to build, and to receive victory. **Hebrews 11:3** states,

"By faith we understand that the [worlds were framed by the word of God, so that the things which are seen were not made of things which are visible."

How amazing! The universe came into existence through speech... the speech of God! As a Believer of Jesus Christ, you must understand that your Words carry power. Learn to use your words to build and to overcome the devil. Michael used his words in one of his fights against Satan,

> *"Yet Michael the archangel, in contending with the devil, when he disputed about the body of Moses, dared not bring against him a reviling accusation, but said, "The Lord rebuke you!"* (**Jude 9**)

Your salvation came through the confession of by words, *"For with the heart one believes unto righteousness, and with the mouth confession is made unto salvation"* (**Romans 10:10**).

> *"When evening had come, they brought to Him many who were demon-possessed. And He cast out the spirits with a word, and healed all who were sick."* – Matthew 8:16

What a wonderful tool for casting out demons and healing the sick. Jesus did it with "a word" out of His mouth. Simply powerful!!! Most of Jesus' healings were through His words rather than touching. Like a growing human being needs to learn in the natural life, you must also learn to and know how to use your words and how to speak the Word of God. One of the greatest gifts afforded to you is the receiving of the gift of tongues. The gift of tongues is the promise that under the New Covenant, we will speak with *"new tongues"* (**Mark 16:17**). Language is an identification of culture. Your speech identifies you with the Kingdom of God.

WALKING

The next phase or level concerning your divine calling of finishing the race is your ability to walk. In the ministry that I have received from God through the grace of the Lord Jesus Christ, a very significant aspect that I have advertently and unwaveringly focused on is the progress of the Believer. A critical part of the assignment given to me by our gracious Lord is to have God's people excel both spiritually and naturally.

> *"Now when they saw the boldness of Peter and John, and perceived that they were uneducated and untrained men, they marveled. And they realized that they had been with Jesus."* - **Acts 4:13**

I believe that no one should be in Christ without progressing holistically. Through the grace of God, I have witnessed many whom the Lord has brought under the grace of my life, transformed in every area of their lives. God did not call you to a stand-still, and neither did He call you to be stagnated. *"For in Him we live and move and have our being"* (**Acts 17:28**). God is God of action. Every time you see the presence of God in

Scripture, He is always doing something and/or moving towards something incredible. Seek and pursue God to grant you the grace of activeness. **Philippians 2:13** says *"for it is God who works in you both to will and to do for His good pleasure."* God wants you to "will" and to "do". Pay careful attention to scripture and you will discover that God never called or used anybody who was initially doing nothing. Abraham, Moses, Amos, the Lord's disciples, Paul, and so on and so forth, were all doing something before God called them and anointed them for their divine purpose. God does not embrace or encourage laziness. The book of Genesis tells us that God worked six out of seven business days. That's an incredible feat from a Being who does not need to work. Scripture says He neither sleep nor slumber (**Psalm 121:2-4**). The aforementioned Scripture actually also says "He watches over Israel". Jesus as we speak is working diligently preparing a place for you and I (**John 14:2**) as we journey to finish our race here on earth.

> *"I say then: Walk in the Spirit, and you shall not fulfill the lust of the flesh."* – **Galatians 5:16**

Walking is what moves you from where you are right now to where you need to be in the next moment. **Galatians 5:16** tells you that if you do not *"walk by the Spirit"*, your flesh will take over your divine assignment.

May the Lord grant you the grace and ability to be a mover in the Spirit. Walking in the Spirit means progressing well in the things of God. A person who walks is always progressing. Walkers are always exercising…walking in the spirit means always exercising your faith for the release of the purpose of God both in your life and on the earth. Walking sprouts growth and advancement. Walk in the Word! Walk in the Spirit! Walk… Walk towards the finishing line!

THE WINE OF THE SPIRIT

Without the Person of the Spirit no one is saved. He is the ONE who draws us in. He is also our only seal of salvation (**Ephesians 1:13; 4:30; 2 Corinthians 1:22**). The Holy Spirit is the guarantee of your salvation, for no one can say (believe) that Jesus is Lord unless by the Spirit (**1 Corinthians 12:3**). Having known this, it is imperative to note that there is a difference between a gift and the giver of the gift. There is a difference between the Person of the Holy Spirit and the gifts He gives (**1 Corinthians chapter 12, 13 and 14**). Upon salvation through the leadership of the Spirit, you the Believer must seek the gift of the Spirit, which is available to you.

> **John 7:38-39** – *"He who believes in Me, as the Scripture has said, out of his heart will flow rivers of living water." But this He spoke concerning the Spirit, whom those [g]believing in Him would receive; for the [h]Holy Spirit was not yet given, because Jesus was not yet glorified."*

*"And do not be drunk with wine, in which is
dissipation; but be filled with the Spirit"*
– **Ephesians 5:18**

The Holy Spirit is the provider of the drink that forever satisfies
and quenches the thirst of the righteousness of God. This same
Spirit is called the "Helper" (**John 14:16; 14:26; 15:26; 16:7**).
The satisfier of your thirst for more of God as a sojourner on a
pilgrimage; helps you navigate this life and advance through your
journey of faith. I have always said, 'it is better to be in the game
than to be in the stands'. 'It is better to be a sheer participator
than to be a mere spectator. The Believer who does not desire for
the gifts of the Spirit is like the player who would rather be on
the bench than on the field of play. Once salvation is received, it
is the duty of the recipient of God's gracious redemption to desire
earnestly for the gifts of the Holy Spirit (**1 Corinthians 12:31,
1 Corinthians 14:1**). The outcome of the Spirit's baptism is the
divine, powerful and awesome experience of the receiving of the
gifts of the Holy Spirit. Being a believer without the baptism of
the Holy Spirit is like being a professional athlete who is never on
the field of play but would rather sit on the bench. The Baptism of
the Holy Spirit awakens you and inspires you throughout the race
of faith. The power of the Holy Spirit helps you in diverse ways
and accordingly as you you progress. The Holy Spirit's baptism
stirs you up with excitement. He gives you a heavenly taste of
divine traits and attributes. If you do not have the experience of
the baptism of the Holy Spirit, desire and seek the gifts. Talk to
your Pastor about it, search the Scriptures about what it means
and how to receive it. Fast and pray for it. Anyone who is born

again is of age to be drunk in the Spirit. It is one thing to be born of the water (Baptism) but it is a whole different level to be born of the Spirit (fire).

> *"John answered, saying to all, "I indeed baptize you with water; but One mightier than I is coming, whose sandal strap I am not worthy to loose. He will baptize you with the Holy Spirit and fire.* [17] *His winnowing fan is in His hand, and He will thoroughly clean out His threshing floor, and gather the wheat into His barn; but the chaff He will burn with unquenchable fire."* - **Luke 3:17-17**

SOLID FOOD

This is one of the most important bearings of the Kingdom of God. Have you ever sat under the most exciting and powerful revelatory teaching of the Word of God? It's called the receiving of solid food. It is where God by His Spirit reveals hidden things of His Word to the Believer. It is the most impacting encounter for the Believer. This is where maturation and growth take place. This is where the Believer learns to overcome while growing. Desiring stronger and growing interest in solid food is a great sign of maturity. As a Pastor, I can attest that there is nothing more exciting than teaching a group of people who are excited about the things of God. It takes understanding and true appreciation for what the Word is worth in order to get to that level in God.

"For though by this time you ought to be teachers, you need someone to teach you again the first principles of the oracles of God; and you have come to need milk and not solid food." – **Hebrews 5:12**

> *"But solid food belongs to those who are of full age, that is, those who by reason of use have their senses exercised to discern both good and evil."*
> - **Hebrews 5:14**

> **"I fed you with milk and not with solid food; for until now you were not able *to receive it*, and even now you are still not able."** - **1 Corinthians 3:2**

Solid food is for the strong and the grown. It does not matter the thickness or the strength it requires, the mature can receive and chew on it. It is the slow process of handling the Word line upon line and precept upon precept. A good steak in most cases requires a slow chumping.

SECRETS OF GOD

There is much to be learnt from Job. Job is one of the best examples in Scripture about the race of faith. The incredible story of Job starts with him living and enjoying the best conditions of life. He went from having it all to losing it all and then having it all in double portions. I have always said in some of my teachings that one of the worst conditions in life is to taste the goodness of riches, becoming accustomed to the enriching lifestyle and then losing it all. The first few verses of the Book are committed to the presentation of his wealth before he lost it all. The Book revealed many things about the walk of faith, God's view on how crisis and difficult seasons of life are to be handled by the Believer, and the ultimate reward of not giving up on your faith. One of the most interesting and revealing parts of the Book was some of the revelations by Job particularly in Chapter 29. In verse 3 and 4, Job said, *"The candle of the Lord is above my head...."*. Here is where the Psalmist would say "selah".... Ponder upon that for a moment. In the midst of the most difficult experience that any human could possibly face, Job's focus was on the candle of the Lord that was casting light over him. He then said, *"The secret of God has been over my tent since my youth'*. No wonder Job made it out of all those remarkable trials. Since Job's life as a youth, God was revealing deep things of the journey of faith to him and it helped propel him to overcome whatever the world, the devil and even his own flesh threw at him. May the candle of the Lord shine upon your head in Jesus Name! May you know the secrets of the Lord in Jesus Name!! **Ephesians 1:9** says God has *"made known to us the mystery of His will, according to His good pleasure which He purposed in Himself"*. You too, if you opened up your heart in receiving the Word of faith, the candle of the Lord will lead you through this life. God has revealed His secrets to you through His Word and by His Spirit. This has been the desire of the Lord since the Old Covenant,

> **Amos 3:7** - *"Surely the Lord GOD does nothing, unless He reveals His secret to His people the prophets."*

The Hebrew word for "prophet" here is nāvî. "Nāvî" means "spokesperson" (not just in the Christian traditional understanding of "prophet", but anyone who is an agent or ambassador for Christ.) God wants to give aid to you through revelation of His secrets. **God wants to tell you what's behind the text of Scripture.** There is Spirit behind the letter (**2 Corinthians 3:6**) that He gladly wants to make known to you. **Daniel (2:20-23)** attested to this by saying **"God reveals deep things…"** My wife and I have both had many experiences where God has revealed things to us before important meetings to help us be adequately prepared. There is a remarkable story in **Genesis (18:16-19).** In these verses, God was getting ready to bring judgment upon Sodom and Gomorrah due to some heinous sins. Although Abraham didn't live in those cities, he had a relative by the name of Lot, who lived there with his family. God in this incident had an interest in Abraham who had an interest in Lot. God asked Himself a unique question pertaining to His decision to bring judgment to the dwelling cities of Lot. He said, *'Shall I hide this from Abraham?'* Wow! Can you imagine the Lord deliberating such a decision not to hide a judgment over a city away from you? God revealed the judgment to Abraham to allow Abraham to get involved in sparing the life of Lot. There are wonderful, solid and amazing things that God wants to tell you to encourage and to bless you and to help you through your journey of the race of faith.

1 Corinthians 2:9-10 says, *"Eye has not seen, nor ear heard, Nor have entered into the heart of man the things which God has prepared for those who love Him."* **But God has revealed them to us through His Spirit. For the Spirit searches all things, yes, the deep things of God."**

There are two implications of God giving a person a secret. 1) For an assignment on this earth and 2) For personal advancement in the walk of faith. God through revelation provides, protects and preserves His people. "Those who dwell in the secret place of the Most High shall abide under the shadow of the Almighty". Like Job, when you carry the solid and deep things of God, you will abide under the shadow of His favourable presence. The Apostle who declared at the end of his journey on earth that he successfully finished his race is said by Peter that he too knew deep things of God.

> **2 Peter 3:15-17** – *"…as also our beloved brother Paul, according to the wisdom given to him, has written to you, [16] as also in all his epistles, speaking in them of these things, in which are some things hard to understand, which untaught and unstable people twist to their own destruction, as they do also the rest of the Scriptures."*

God has great things to tell you! Paul revealed in **2 Corinthians 12** that God took him to "paradise" and "the third heaven" and showed him things that are impossible for words to describe. God does not have any intention to hide anything from you in this new and better covenant (**Hebrews 8:6**). The solid food of God makes you mature. It means God can rely on you with His secrets. Jesus in **Matthew 16:13-20** asked His disciples whom others were saying He was. After many different opinions, Jesus then intriguingly asked the disciples whom they thought He was. It was a question that required an accurate answer from a person who knew the secrets of God. In that moment, the disciples were accustomed to knowing Jesus to be a Rabbi who did great wonders and a very good teacher. Following Jesus' question, Peter uttered something powerful. He had known a secret of God that none of the rest knew. Peter declared that Jesus is *"the Christ, the Son of the Living God"*. Jesus in the affirmative responded by saying that there was no way Peter would have known that on his own. In fact, Jesus said, *"flesh and blood did not reveal this to you"*, noting that it takes the revelation of the secrets of God to know something as profound as that. Peter had a secret that set him apart. That is what the secret of the Lord does for the Believer. The

Word of God to the Believer is hidden secrets; a mystery revealed. A secret is indeed a mystery of God. It becomes a revelation once it's revealed. Mysteries are secrets hidden from others. Revelations are secrets made manifest to a person. It is recorded more than 25 times in the New Testament that Jesus often went to a solitary place to speak to the Father. There are only three occasions where Jesus' conversation with the Father was revealed to us. When praying for Himself, the disciples and for all of us. In John chapter 17, His prayer in the Garden of Gethsemane before His death on the cross, and lastly when He called out to God while dying on the cross. The Psalms also revealed some aspects of His conversation with the Father such as *"The Lord said to my Lord, sit at My right hand until I make Your enemies Your footstool"* in **Psalm 110:1** and affirmed by the Lord in **Matthew 22:44**. Other than these examples, the things spoken between Jesus and the Father were secrets between them just as **2 Corinthians 12** were secrets between Paul and the Lord. Think about this.... Moses spent a lot of time before God. God warned Aaron and Miriam to be watchful concerning Moses because among all the people of the earth, He spoke only with Moses face to face. *"Then He said, "Hear now My words: If there is a prophet among you, I, the LORD, make Myself known to him in a vision; I speak to him in a dream. Not so with My servant Moses; he is faithful in all My house. I speak with him face to face, even plainly, and not in [d]dark sayings; and he sees the form of the LORD. Why then were you not afraid To speak against My servant Moses?"* – **Numbers 12:6-8**

Although Moses spent many moments before God; forty days in one of those moments... Moses related only a few of those moments (information) to the people; the rest was between him and God. Jesus in most cases will preach in parables but will give His direct followers more. God loves giving those He loves hidden things. These hidden gems are meant to help you with your purpose on this earth. In **Matthew 13:10-11** the disciples asked Jesus *"why do you speak to them in parables?"* He said to them, *"Because it has been given to you to know the mysteries of the kingdom of heaven, but to them it has not been given."*

> **Psalm 25:14** says *"The secret of the LORD is with those who fear Him, and He will show them His covenant."*

The Word of God and the Holy Spirit is your source of direct and undeniable secrets of God. God will use these two to speak to you as you walk this path. In **John 16:12** Jesus said, **"I have much to tell you"**, which is His Word. He then said the rest will come from **"the Holy Spirit"**. In **Jeremiah 33:3** Scriptures says, *'Call to Me, and I will answer you, and show you great and [b]mighty things, which you do not know.'*

May the Lord answer you when you call on Him in Jesus Name! May deep secrets of God give you wisdom; may He strengthen you to be an overcomer. May He continuously make you a true disciple. May His precious anointing make you a witnessing agent. May He give you assurance of God's provision, protection and preservation in Jesus Name!

STANDING

Here, I want to briefly touch on the importance of standing in the faith. Once a baby is born and with proper nutrition and care, the baby must then go through the fundamental process of growth. In due time the baby must learn to stand. This is also the case for babes in Christ. At some point, every Believer must either learn to stand or must go through the phase of standing in the faith. Scripture uses the word "stand" to demonstrate the ability to remain firm. To stand is the faculty to rise and remain on your feet; to pose in an upright position. When you assume the action of "stand", you are representing something. In Christ, you are representing Him as His disciple. To stand in the faith means you are adhering to His divine principles. It also means you will not allow the darts of the devil, the world or your own flesh to get in the way of your faith in Christ. You must learn to stand firm against the waging storm of this life. Cheap things come cheap. Sometimes you must learn to hold on strong and tight on the horns of the altar of sacrifice in order to override the predicament of this world. Standing in the faith is good for your well-being and for your victory. Learn to stand firm! Don't allow the wind of false doctrine and the evil agenda of Satan to blow away your faith in Jesus Christ. Be strong in the Lord. Be visible in the Kingdom, and most importantly stand to the end because **"those who endures to the end shall be saved"** (Matthew 24:13). At this point, I want to ask you a question. For the sake of this point, let's just say everyone you know as a Believer, starts to give up their faith in Jesus. Let us say, your close friends and loved ones who walk in the journey with you start to find their own reason not to serve Christ anymore. Would you still remain in the faith? How about if those people were Believers that you trusted and were influencers in your life? Would you still have the strength and the agility to follow Jesus? Let us just say, some of those were church leaders who are beginning to have a change of heart about the Gospel of Jesus? What if one of them was a Pastor that you trusted? What if they started to not live for Christ anymore? Would you still be able to stand? This is how important learning to stand in the faith is about. Being able to stand firm under any situation, predicament or trials. Being able to stand against the deception of Satan, the pressures of falsehood, the spirit of this age, and against the various darts of the devil. The enemies of your progress in God will try but a standing Believer never gives up or gives in. You have discovered the Truth. You know that the Truth is a Person, and that Person is the Lord Jesus Christ. You must hold on to Him no matter what. You must be unmovable not according to your own strength but through relying on the unchanging arm of Jesus and His Word.

> *"Stand therefore, having girded your waist with truth, having put on the breastplate of righteousness"* – **Ephesians 6:14**

Seek to grow earnestly into knowing how to stand before the Lord in prayer and with supplication. Learn to stand on His Word of Truth. You must learn to stand against the devil and his schemes.

> *"Therefore take up the whole armor of God, that you may be able to withstand in the evil day, and having done all, to stand."* – **Ephesians 6:13**

The preceding verse (13) says once you have completed the wearing of the whole armor of God, the last action to take is to stand. To "stand" is the position to take when you represent someone or something. In your case, you represent God. You are an ambassador for Christ (**2 Corinthians 5:20**) and therefore Christ's agent on this earth. You also represent the Kingdom of God.

Standing is a strong indication that you have already made up your mind and are secured in your decision to follow Jesus. It means you are content as a partaker of the heavenly calling and there is nothing that the devil can do about that. **Colossians 4:12** says, *"that you may stand perfect and complete in all the will of God."*

"Therefore, brethren, stand fast and hold the traditions which you were taught, whether by word or our epistle." - **2 Thessalonians 2:15**. Here, standing means you believe in the strength of the Gospel and upholds the authenticity of the Word of God. You know that God's Word is the truth.

FLYING

Evidently "flying" is out of the ordinary for humans. Although humans are God's favored creation, flying was not one of the attributes afforded to humans without an actual flying object like an airplane. Having mentioned that, Scriptures speak of soaring like eagles in describing the metaphorical abilities of those who put their trust in God.

> *"Those who wait on the LORD shall renew their strength; they shall mount up with wings like eagles, they shall run and not be weary, they shall walk and not faint."*

The above Scripture was declared by the prophet Isaiah (40:31) in relation to the possible heights of those whose strength is in the Lord. This Scripture notably applies to your life on earth. When you have Faith in God's Word, all things are possible (**Luke 1:37; 18:27; Matthew 19:26**). Indeed, with God all things are possible. Although the idea of flying as human is beyond reason, we Believers are going to be given the ability to experience that when we are caught up in the heavens. Yes, the same God who caused the birds, and angels to travel through the sky is going to afford every Believer; whether dead or alive to be caught up through the heavens, faster than any flying creature. Think about this… if no creature had the ability or if there weren't any flying animals that existed; and such creatures were told to you, would you have believed it? Most likely not. Now, we see all sorts of flying creatures, which we are accustomed to because we know they exist. Well, the same God who created them and gave them the ability to fly says there is a day coming when all Believers whether dead or alive will experience the same. Even though Jesus did many great miracles and wonders including walking on water, flying would have been a strange thing to His disciples and yet, when He resurrected, He was taken up to heaven as though He was an angel or even a flying creation. Do you believe in the Word of God? Do you really believe that with God all things are possible? Do you believe that God is the Creator of the eagle, and all other flying creatures? Do you believe that Enoch and Elisha were truly caught up in the heavens? Then you better believe that one day this is going to be you the Believer. The only requirement for you is not giving up on your faith in God through His beloved and righteous Son Jesus Christ, and running the race of faith until the end. There are many confused critics who have twisted and confused otherwise simple Scriptures to mean different things other than being caught up in the heavens but do not be swayed by their assertion and misinterpretation of Scripture. When seeking understanding on a subject matter, it is important to use Scripture to interpret Scripture and allow the Word of God to speak to your heart particularly concerning this subject. Whether dead or alive, all believers will be caught up into the heavens.

"For this we say to you by the word of the Lord, that we who are alive and remain until the coming of the Lord will by no means precede those who are asleep. For the Lord Himself will descend from heaven with a shout, with the voice of an archangel, and with the trumpet of God. And the dead in Christ will rise first. Then we who are alive and remain shall be caught up together with them in the clouds to meet the Lord in the air. And thus we shall always be with the Lord. Therefore comfort one another with these words. - 1 Thessalonians 4:15-18*

The Apostle Paul says knowing and believing the catch away is comforting to the Believer. With all the nonsense and junk happening on this earth, the catch away is comforting to Believers. The Greek word for the term "rapture", which derives from **1 Thessalonians 4:17** is translated "caught up." The Latin translation of the same Scripture used the word "rapturo". The Greek word is also translated "harpazo", which means to snatch or take away. The term is used to describe how the Spirit caught up Philip and brought him to Caesarea (**Acts 8:39**). The same term is used to describe Paul's experience of being caught up into the third heaven (**2 Corinthians 12:2-4**). This is the surety and the everlasting hope of all who walk in the path that Philip, Paul, Elijah, Enoch all walked. As I am writing this book, I just came from a powerful weekend of Good Friday and Resurrection Sunday weekend. The excitement of seeing souls come to Christ during the Good Friday service altar-call and to start their personal and wonderful journey of faith with the Saviour Jesus

Christ, is still brewing in my spirit. Coupled with the thematic preaching of the power of the Resurrection at the Sunday service is just too wonderful to experience and to behold. The experience is unimaginable to those who will deny and reject Christ. To have such great hope in knowing that the source of the existence of the universe and the creator of life is your Father who has opened up a personal relationship with you through the grace and the ultimate sacrifice of His only begotten Son Jesus. I cannot wait to behold Him above the clouds.

> *"Behold, I tell you a ᶦmystery: We shall not all sleep, but we shall all be changed in a moment, in the twinkling of an eye, at the last trumpet. For the trumpet will sound, and the dead will be raised incorruptible, and we shall be changed. For this corruptible must put on incorruption, and this mortal must put on immortality. So when this corruptible has put on incorruption, and this mortal has put on immortality, then shall be brought to pass the saying that is written: "Death is swallowed up in victory.""* **1 Corinthians 15:51-54**

Enoch, Elijah and Jesus are all examples that this is going to happen. It is beyond exciting just to think about it. There are one of two ways for the believer to transition into eternity… either you are individually called home into eternal glory or corporately with those remaining on this earth at the sound of the trumpet. The rapture is an act into eternal glory. The "flying away" will be our last port between this natural life and eternity. In Paul's letter to the young Pastor Timothy at the church in Ephesus, Paul assured the church of two promises. In Chapter 4:8, he asserted that we have two promises in Christ, one which now is, and another to come. The former speaks about the gracious relationship we have with God now. A relationship affords us the right to be called the children of God by faith.

> *"He came to His own, and His own did not receive Him. [12] But as many as received Him, to them He gave the right to become children of God, to those who believe in His name: [13] who were born, not of blood, nor of the will of the flesh, nor of the will of man, but of God."* John 1:11-13

To be able to pray to the everlasting and all powerful God. The grace to work in miracle and to be able to call upon Him on this earth is a great fulfilling promise. The former in Paul's statement speaks of another... Here, he speaks of an eternal blessing after life on this earth. If this does not get you excited I don't know what will. Scriptures dedicate many passages of Christ to assure you of this pending trip to glory. Many gamble their life for the worse but those who have accepted Christ have received a surety of a better Kingdom. Get ready, pack up, and look up! Behold He comes!

YOU SHOULD KNOW

1 John 2:26-27 – "These things I have written to you concerning those who try to [f]deceive you. 27 But the anointing which you have received from Him abides in you, and you do not need that anyone teach you; but as the same anointing teaches you concerning all things, and is true, and is not a lie, and just as it has taught you, you [g]will abide in Him."

The Apostle John here, is not requesting that Believer become unteachable, uneducable or proud. The subject and the context are concerning deception. There is a caution to all Believers regarding being deceived away from the faith. You are urged as a Believer to be vigilant. The Apostle assures that the anointing in you carries the capability of deciphering truth from deception when you allow God to be who He is in your life. As a believer, you should have enough of the Word of God in you. You must be sensitive to the Spirit who is also your Anointer, so that when you are encountered with deceiving thoughts, ideas, interpretation or philosophy, you know enough to be bold in standing against the deception. You are a Believer in Jesus Christ, you are an offspring of the living God and you have a future filled with the hope that is sure and steadfast. It is important that you have unmovable faith concerning this truth. When you know and believe this truth concerning your life here on earth, divine excitement will grow and reside in you. You will begin to look forward to the glorious appearance of Jesus; knowing that you are blessed both on this earth and most importantly in the one to come.

> **Titus 2:11-15**
>
> *"For the grace of God that brings salvation has appeared to all men, teaching us that, denying ungodliness and worldly lusts, we should live soberly, righteously, and godly in the present age, <u>looking for the blessed hope and glorious appearing of our great God and Savior Jesus Christ</u>, who gave Himself for us, that He might redeem us from every lawless deed and purify for Himself His own special people, zealous for good works. Speak these things, exhort, and rebuke with all authority. Let no one despise you."*

> **2 Timothy 4:6-8**
>
> *"For I am already being poured out as a drink offering, and the time of my departure is at hand. I have fought the good fight, I have finished the race, I have kept the faith. Finally, there is laid up for me the crown of righteousness, which the Lord, the righteous Judge, <u>will give to me on that Day,</u>*

and not to me only but also to all who have loved His appearing."

In my life as a Believer of Jesus Christ, I have seen some "Christians" claim that we are still sinners even after salvation. Sometimes these assertions are an impression of "humility" by the claimants. What these individuals mean is that, we are born-again with sin tendencies. The first time that the word sin appeared in Scriptures, God told Adam that sin will always lie at his door. Meaning, as long as humans are on this earth, sin will always be around.

"sin lies at the door. And its desire is for you, but you should rule over it." (**Genesis 4:7**).

This incident was not the first sin committed by a human in Scripture but it was the first description of the intention of sin. God spoke these words to Cain after he had taken the life of his own brother due to envy and jealousy. Sin will always lie at the door of humans but those saved are saved from sin.

2 Corinthians 5:21 says *"For He made Him who knew no sin to be sin for us, that we might become the righteousness of God in Him."*

Jesus has already died and made you righteous before God. There are no ifs ands or buts. The blood of Jesus has made you whole. Paul was human like you, who also needed salvation and yet upon his salvation and upon finishing his race on this earth, he said,

"I have fought the good fight, I have finished the race, I have kept the faith. [8] Finally, there

**is laid up for me the crown of righteousness,
which the Lord, the righteous Judge, will give
to me on that Day, and not to me only but also
to all who have loved His appearing."
2 Timothy 4:7-8**

Not only did Paul know that he was saved, he also said boldly that he is going to receive a reward from the faithful God. Just because you have sin tendencies as a human doesn't mean you are not righteous before God. It is Jesus who makes you righteous. 2 Corinthians 5:21 says, *"For He made Him who knew no sin to be sin for us, that we might become the righteousness of God in Him."*

Your sin tendency reminds you that you are still living in carnal flesh. The good news is, God through Jesus has made you righteous, and has given you the His holy Word (Scripture) and His Holy Spirit to help you overcome the power of sin.

CONCLUSION

"Therefore we also, since we are surrounded by so great a cloud of witnesses, let us lay aside every weight, and the sin which so easily ensnares us, and let us run with endurance the race that is set before us, looking unto Jesus, the [a]author and [b] finisher of our faith, who for the joy that was set before Him endured the cross, despising the shame, and has sat down at the right hand of the throne of God." – **Hebrews 12:1-2**

"But he who endures to the end shall be saved."
– **Matthew 24:13**

You must endeavour to have the above Scripture be your encouragement, your incentive and your inspiration! Your encouragement is highly important to God. In some of the Scriptures quoted in this book, we see that the Lord, mostly through the Apostle Paul, encourages you to be comforted by the declaration of eternal hope. Unlike those who build their house on a sinking sand by putting their trust in this departing world and in material things, you have established and built your life on Jesus the Rock. Your hope is in the Creator and not the created. Your source of future is in the Creator rather than in creation. Your eternal life is certain! Cheer up! No matter where a person is in life and no matter what they have accomplished, they are still lost without Jesus. There is no amount of duration on this earth and no accumulation of pleasure that can measure up to the eternal bliss of heaven. The life of the oldest person to have ever lived on this earth is still a dot in eternity. Comfort yourself with the Word of God that assures anyone who believes in Jesus of eternal life. The same God who afforded life on this earth has promised a better and eternal one. The condition of entering into this world was ordained by God and the same God has created a condition for the eternal life that He gives. That condition is faith in His Son Jesus Christ. You have hope. There is coming a time in the eternal future where sickness, pain, sorrow, death, and all other earthly impediments will be erased forever, it will be gone with the wind of the Holy Spirit. The God who allowed humans to discover some process of healing to the body will destroy infirmities forever. God has appointed tremendous blessings for you on this earth; He has also declared an eternal life for you.

As you journey through your personal and respective faith, may our heavenly Father through His beloved Son, Jesus Christ ignite your faith to grow and glow beyond reach. May the Spirit and the power of His Word infuse you with supernatural strength. May you excel and create a lasting impact on those who know you and beyond. May your life be an example to those who will come after you just as the lives of those who were mentioned in **Hebrews 11** is touching your life. May you increase in the anointing and fulfil your purpose. May you gloriously finish the race in Jesus Name!!!